Data Strategies for Data Governance

CREATING A PRAGMATIC, AGILE, AND
COMMUNICABLE FOUNDATION FOR YOUR DATA
MANAGEMENT PRACTICE

Marilu Lopez

Technics Publications
SEDONA, ARIZONA

Published by:

115 Linda Vista, Sedona, AZ 86336 USA

https://www.TechnicsPub.com

Edited by Laura Sebastian-Coleman

Cover design by Christian Inchaustegui

First Printing 2023

Copyright © 2023 by María Guadalupe López Flores

ISBN, print ed.   9781634623797

ISBN, Kindle ed.   9781634623803

ISBN, ePub ed.   9781634623810

ISBN, PDF ed.   9781634623827

Library of Congress Control Number: 2023940653

To my Mom, who keeps looking after me from the other side of the clouds. She put on my way two angels that made a dream team: Danette McGilvray, my sherpa in this journey, and Laura Sebastian-Coleman, my best English teacher.

To Miguel, Omar, and Adrian for their lovely support. Together we'll always have the force of MMOA.

To my extended family and friends for their cheering words through this journey.

A dream doesn't become reality through magic; it takes sweat, determination and hard work.

Colin Powell

PRAISE FOR
DATA STRATEGIES FOR DATA GOVERNANCE

We all know that data will play an increasingly important role in all future operations. How you personally and your organization apply data to operations will be the difference between success and failure. Have worked in this area for many years, the time is ripe for the next step in the evolution of data strategy. Marilu has taken this step. As an enthusiastic adherent to the business canvas technique, I greatly admire the diligence with which she has applied this to the concept of formulating a data strategy. There is a wealth of material in this very dense book of extremely useful tips, techniques, and guidance. Probably the most difficult aspect of data strategy formulation centers on the challenge of meaningfully engaging various stakeholders in the necessary dialogs required to take your organizations data and applying it meaningfully in support of the organizational strategy. The method described provides all the guidance you will need.

Peter Aiken
President, DAMA International

This is a comprehensive book on data strategies. Marilu Lopez has come up with a way to connect the data strategy to executive management that until now has been a missing piece; how to set the data strategies in motion. She doesn't just go into how to create a data strategy as if it were a cake to be baked. Instead, she makes the reader think about what kind of data strategies are needed and how they fit into your organization's challenges, intentions, and aspirations. The content is very credible as Marilu Lopez consistently uses and relates to academic research, literature, and thought leaders' experiences. Thus, her PAC framework is based on today's accumulated knowledge and takes you further from there. If you are about to take on data strategy work, you should start by first checking out Marilu Lopez's messages.

Håkan Edvinsson
CTO, Principal Consultant, Informed Decisions

Marilu Lopez' book is an important addition to the canon of Data Governance. Many books showcase 'the what' and 'the why' - this book teaches you 'the how' of building a successful program. The first section targets business leaders and does an excellent job of educating non-technical people with the importance of a Data Governance program. But the real value is providing a detailed road map, with practical tools for practitioners to use, to deliver program deliverables - and capture, demonstrate, and communicate the value.

Highly recommended!

Charles Harbour
Data Governance Program Manager at HP

Today's college graduates think that technology is all about choosing a technology or a technology stack in order to get work done. They don't see that there is a larger infrastructure that they are a part of. What is needed is a book on the larger concepts that shape the IT industry. I recommend the book by Marilu Lopez as a starting place for understanding the larger framework under which IT operates.

Bill Inmon
CEO of Forest Rim Technology

You had me at "Pragmatic, Agile, and Communicable." One of the perceptions of Data Management is that we are slow, overly complicated, and use convoluted terms and ideas. This work shows that it's entirely possible to define a data strategy that is understandable and usable by all the stakeholders: executives, management, knowledge workers, developers, and data professionals. Marilu lays out everything you need to add data value to your organization, tailored to your industry and organizational culture. I look forward to applying the PAC Method to my future projects.

Karen Lopez
Sr. Project Manager, InfoAdvisors

Marilu has produced a valuable and detailed tour-de-force in this very comprehensive guide to developing an enterprise-level Data Strategy that is pragmatic, agile, and communicable. It is clear that she recognizes, from her own extensive experience, that most organizations have not been able to muster the engagement and collaboration needed to produce whole-of-organization agreements about how to articulate and align the key components, that is, data management, technology, architecture, and governance.

The challenge that she set herself, and has mastered, is HOW to harness business interests in the light of the current and future data landscape and technology opportunities. Her 10-step Data Strategy Cycle is fully elucidated, and each activity and sub-activity, with its corresponding goals and objectives, is fully described. No thoughtful reader will be able to conclude that any level of instruction – who, why, what, when, and how – has been neglected. Throughout the chapters, charts, and diagrams summarize the proposed method effectively. Since my experiences have taught me that every organization, from a huge conglomerate to a new startup, benefits from conducting a Data Management Assessment, it was gratifying to see that as a foundational requirement as Part 1, Step 2, very early in the strategy lifecycle.

In my data management courses over the last decade, one of the main team exercises is outlining a data management strategy because it pulls together the component disciplines of data management and encourages enterprise-level thinking, which is vital for a Chief Data Officer. In addition, Marilu de-mystifies the crucial task of decomposing the business strategy and aligning it to data – domains, architecture, and governance. The final step in this phase is developing Key Performance Indicators, enabling executives to measure progress towards the strategic goals of the business. The Data Strategy development phases she describes collectively encompass a systematic, consistent home for every key element of what it takes to manage data assets effectively.

The Data Strategy Canvases are not only a useful mechanism to unpack complexity bite by bite, gaining agreement every step of the way, but also lend themselves as a proof-of-concept trial of ownership and stewardship roles, which are then planned and implemented through an integrated, multi-leveled roadmap.

Participants in the development of the Data Strategy will broaden and deepen their understanding of data across the organization and learn their responsibilities from the ground up. Along the way, Marilu addresses and clarifies several of our industry's 'terms of art,' such as "data-driven," "data literacy" and "digital transformation." And she employs a rational, functional approach to answering the perennial question we often hear at conferences "What is the difference between data management and data governance?" The reader will receive an evidence-based answer in this book, as she meticulously describes roles and responsibilities wedded to phases and strategy development tasks.

If your organization has recognized the need to create a Data Strategy, I highly recommend this book! (No excuses, people, you can do it).

Melanie Mecca
CEO & Principal EDM Expert
DataWise, Inc.

Data Strategy is a cornerstone to building the path to an evolving, matured Data Management practice. The maturity of the process to define it evolves over time. Marilu has captured this in an attainable process that embeds the Data Strategy into Business Strategic Planning in an evolving cycle.

Mike Meriton
Enterprise Data Management Council
Co-Founder and COO EDM Council

This engaging book captures a terrific collection of guidance, templates and methods. These would be very useful to develop and support data management capabilities for a broad range of business types in varying degrees of maturity. There are excellent samples and narration for data management professionals through the journey with a constant eye on how to align with business strategies – helping to answer 'the why would they care' question. There are relevant scenarios described and ideas for how to handle many situations along your road to success. The most compelling artifacts throughout are the canvas samples, which can be easy-to-use visuals, that thread together a full process and flow, while keeping each document readable and consumable. The PAC acronym of Pragmatic, Agile and Communicable captures the essence of this book. The approach is practical, useable, and relevant. It is agile in that there is a built-in flexibility to how you can use it and evolve your business and data management capabilities together. Lastly communicable – is realized so well through the assorted styles of canvases. The interviews throughout the book align with the necessity to pair up business strategies and make for additional understanding of the need for something so practical in many companies. I highly recommend this as a guiding tool for anyone trying to advance their organization through Data Management Maturity.

Dawn Michels
DAMA International Board
Presidents' Council Chair

The thing I liked the best about Marilu Lopez's book on Data Strategy was the "P" (Pragmatic) in her PAC Method. Instead of a lot of theory, this book gives practical ideas on how to either start or enhance an Enterprise's Data Strategy. Marilu's conversational tone makes it easy to understand the different types of strategies an organization should implement under the umbrella of "Data Management." The interviews with experts give the reader practical advice gained from their years of experience working with diverse organizations and will also reveal that there is more to Data Management than gathering and organizing data. First, you need a comprehensive plan--the PAC Method.

As Melanie Mecca says in her interview, "Basically, data is forever; you need to manage it effectively forever...". The PAC method, with its understandable graphs and tables, meets the challenge of implementing a lasting data structure that will contribute to new technologies and new tools and even withstand the onslaught of Artificial Intelligence.

Catherine Nolan
Board Member, DAMA International

A direct method full of practical steps of how to design proper Data Strategies for any organization. This book responds to the "How" we can align Business Objectives with Data Strategies using a set of key deliverables. A must-read book for any data professional targeting to assume a data leadership role.

CDMP Diego Palacios
Founder & President DAMA Perú Chapter

At last, we seem to be reaching a consensus that our data, information, and knowledge are valuable. The term "Information Asset" is gaining currency. A global wine company has taken simple steps to realize the value of its Information Assets through two separate exercises. In the first exercise, by developing and implementing some simple instruments, including a file plan and naming conventions, the organization drove a productivity improvement of $10,800 per person per year, about a 10% performance improvement. The Winery Manager said, "There is no other project in our entire investment portfolio that could have delivered a greater result, more quickly, with better staff satisfaction." In the second exercise, the organization valued and sold harvest and yield data, *achieving a 1,200% return on investment over 3 years and a break-even of 13 weeks. As we, the Data Leaders, say in the Manifesto, "Your organization's best opportunities for organic growth lie in data.*

We are also made regularly and painfully aware that our data, information, and knowledge are vulnerable. In an unpleasant example, it was reported that a recent data breach had cost Australia's second-largest telecommunications provider 10% of its mobile customers, and "56 percent of current customers are considering changing telcos". And an even more recent data breach of Australia's largest private health insurer has wiped nearly $2 billion off its market capitalization.

Whether we are managing risk, driving business outcomes or both, it pays us to manage our data well. So how do we do that? We start by developing and properly implementing a data strategy. This is more than airy words and vague intentions. It's more than shiny new software tools. Marilu has written an easy to understand, step by step and artifact supported method on how to define data strategies. This is a valuable resource that guides us in how to value and protect our most vital assets, our data, information, and knowledge. I recommend The Data Strategy PAC Method to anyone who is serious about doing so.

James Price
CEO and Founder Experience Matters

For decades, data professionals have been advised to "get closer to the business" and to "connect business and data strategy," But how? Finally, a book that answers this question! Well done, Marilu Lopez!

Tom Redman
"The Data Doc." Data Quality Solutions

*In her book, **Marilu Lopez** takes "Data Strategy" to a new level. Having more than 20 years of experience in data governance and management, she is able to take **Data Strategy** from Idealistic to pragmatic, from loose to precise, and from theoretical to practical. The **PAC Method** will guide you step-by-step toward the successful implementation of a data strategy (or strategies, as you will learn when you read the book). It is a must-read for data professionals coveting "competitive advantage" in managing "data assets" in their companies by having and implementing a robust Data Strategy.*

Alejandro Rejon
Data Governance Professional | DAMA CDMP | ISO 8000 Master Data Quality Manager
Certified | M.Sc. Finance

A delightful guide about designing sound data strategies in an effective way. In this book, Marilu brightly bridges an important gap, gracefully displaying all her knowledge, experience, and intelligence by simplifying one of the most complex tasks in data management, creating a sound and achievable data strategy. I have already put to work many of the guidelines detailed in the method, and I am certain it will be a tremendous aid for institutions that find defining and achieving long-term strategies an impossible dream, especially in Latin America.

David Rivera
Academic Development VP, DAMA Ecuador Chapter

Marilu has married two big ideas. First, she illustrates how a data strategy is an umbrella under which other targeted strategies sit. Second, she shows how to use Canvases to create 1-page summaries that every staff member can carry with them into execution work. It's a simple but information-rich and very practical approach. Bravo!!!

Gwen Thomas
Founder, The Data Governance Institute and Principal, DGI Consulting

Contents

Figures

Tables

About the Author

Marilu Lopez (María Guadalupe López Flores, a Mexican-US Citizen born in Los Angeles, California, but raised in Mexico City from age 4) dedicated over 30 years to corporate life in the financial sector before becoming a Data Management consultant and trainer. She pioneered the Enterprise Architecture practice in Mexico, which led her to focus on Data Architecture and, from there, expand her practice to Data Management, specializing in Data Governance, Metadata Management, and Data Quality Management. Through decades she suffered the lack of a holistic and comprehensive Data Strategy. Her passion for Data Management has moved her to dedicate her volunteer work to DAMA International with different roles, from being president of the DAMA Mexico Chapter to becoming VP of Chapter Services.

In her role as entrepreneur Marilu is the founder and CEO of SEGDA (Servicios de Estrategia y Gestión de Datos Applicada – Strategy and Applied Data Management Services). This Mexican company is targeted to contribute to educating data professionals and support organizations on the journey of managing their data to get value out of it through defining Data Strategies and implementing Operating Models.

Acknowledgments

With no doubt, this book couldn´t have been a reality without the coincidence in time and space of three key people to whom I will always have a debt: Danette, Laura, and Steve.

I will never forget that lunch at DGIQ 2021 in San Diego. Among the joy of an in-person meeting after the Covid-19 pandemic, meeting with good and admired friends and sharing the table with Danette McGilvray. It was amazing; in what was an informal and unplanned chat, I told her about my dream of writing a book someday. Only some minutes passed before she was on my side, giving me guidance on how to write a book. I couldn't be more grateful for all she has taught me about how to write a book and how to get it published. Not only did I receive all this valuable guidance from her, but a continuous cheering, overall when I thought this work was useless. Her priceless mentoring inspires me to share my proposal with the wide data community, hoping this seed can reach unimaginable places to contribute to a world with better data.

Although being born in the US, my mother tongue has always been Spanish. One of my biggest challenges was to write this book in English to be able to share it with Data Management thought leaders and get their feedback. I had met Laura Sebastian-Coleman in 2019, when she was invited to speak at DAMA Mexico Chapter annual conference. I learned how kind and accessible she is. This moved me to send her my book project proposal to explore if she thought it could interest readers. When I got her editing of my proposal, I was impressed by the level of detail, insight, and value of her feedback. She was very kind to edit my book. When I worked in the coordination and editing of the DMBoK 2nd Edition translation to Spanish, I remember thinking about the hard work she did editing it. Work I do not envy at all. The second priceless gift life gave me in this journey was having the support of Laura. She has not only been the best English teacher I could ever imagine. She represents the valuable combination of being an English expert and a Data Management thought leader.

Even with the marvelous support of Danette and Laura, you wouldn't be reading this if Steve Hoberman hadn't trusted this work. When working on the DMBoK 2nd Edition translation to Spanish, I learned how pragmatic Steve is. This is something I deeply admire about him. This made me feel confident that my dream could come true. So, thank you, Steve, for trusting me and my work.

Life has given me the fortune to meet people with vast experience in Data Management and real thought leaders, from whom I have learned most of what I know in this fascinating data world. I remember meeting Bill Inmon in the early 1990s. He was giving advice in the bank I worked in about our data warehouse. He told me something I will never forget: "If you pick a report and you are not able to tell where the data came from, you are not managing your data." Twenty-nine years later, this memory moved me to invite him to the last DAMA Mexico Chapter annual conference I organized. I was impressed when he immediately responded and accepted. The experience was unforgettable. I'm grateful and honored for his immediate response to the interview, but overall, for his friendship.

A few people have asked me why I dedicate so much time of my life to my volunteer work at DAMA International. My answer is that I get a very high payback in the form of all the experience I have earned and the great people I have been able to meet. At the second annual conference of the DAMA Mexico Chapter, we invited Tom Redman and James Price, and I learned so much from them. The practical way to teach Data Quality from Tom, and the wonderful story behind Experience Matters from James have inspired me greatly. Thank you both for accepting to be part of this book through the Data Strategy Interviews.

It was at the first DAMA Mexico Chapter conference that we had Melanie Mecca as an invited speaker. I remember the excitement I had to be sitting for dinner with the director of the Data Management Maturity Model I had been using at work. Adopting a Data Management Maturity Model is an essential piece for The Data Strategy PAC Method, so I had to ask Melanie what her experience was with Data Strategy. Thank you, Melanie, for accepting to participate and supporting my findings on the impact of lacking Data Strategy.

San Diego DGIQ 2021 was the scenario where I met David Plotkin, whom I have referenced so many times in my classes. I remember chatting with him aside DAMA International booth. I told him about my book and that I would like to have his point of view on Data Strategy. He agreed to be interviewed. Thanks for that, David, and for your constructive feedback.

There is one approach on Data Governance that I very much like. This is the Data Diplomacy from Håkan Edvinsson. The idea of moving from a coercive model to a Data Governance based on principles and extending the influence of this function beyond data policies caught my attention immediately. I very much enjoyed chatting with Håkan during the interview and confirming we had coincidences in the way we saw Data Strategy. Thank you, Håkan.

The strongest motivation I had to write this book came from the positive feedback I received from the audiences when talking about The Data Strategy PAC Method at EDW and DGIQ conferences, so a special THANK YOU goes to Tony Shaw for giving me the opportunity to share my ideas.

Several works inspired this one. I want to thank Donna Burbank for her openness in letting me reference her Data Strategy Framework.

The most powerful inspiration I had came from the Business Model Canvas, so thank you, Alex Osterwalder, for creating it and spreading it worldwide.

All the ideas I put together to produce The Data Strategy PAC Method would not have any value if they weren't applied in real life in different organizations. I'm especially grateful to my former mates in the adventure of living the method in the first organizations, Ramon Hernandez and Christian Vazquez, colleagues I met when founding DAMA Mexico Chapter. Thank you, Ramon, for finding opportunities to apply the methodology.

During the journey of writing this book, I found a great cheerleader. A Mexican living in Australia, who became my earliest reader. He provided very good feedback from a common reader perspective, being a Data Governance practitioner. Thank you, Alex Rejon!

I wouldn't be on this path if I hadn't learned about DAMA International. I'm more than grateful to this amazing organization and to all its past and present Board members I've met, for giving me great experiences.

To all my other beta readers, Gwen Thomas, Cathy Nolan, Karen Lopez, Dawn Michels, Charles Harbour, Diego Palacios, David Rivera, Peter Aiken, and Mike Meriton, thank you for dedicating your time to going through my book and a big THANKS for your kind and supportive words. It makes me feel that all the effort was worth doing it.

I had the fortune to have someone in my way to capture the essence of my work in the book's cover design, Christian Inchaustegui. Thank you, Peech! I can't miss Aaron Torres and Carlos Sanchez, who created this book's web companion site. They are all part of the amazing Treehouse Marketing team led by Omar Perez. Thank you all!

Last but never least, a big THANK YOU to Miguel, my beloved partner in so many ways, for his special way of cheering me.

Foreword

If you haven't heard of Marilu Lopez, let me be the first to introduce her! Marilu is well known in the data management community in Mexico, having co-founded and served as an officer of DAMA Mexico. She is also known internationally for her extensive work on the DAMA International board (DAMA being Data Management Association). Her years working in the financial sector and now on her own as a consultant give her deep expertise in data management. She understands foundational concepts and has real-life experience successfully implementing those ideas. You can be confident that she has the credentials to author this book.

Over lunch at the December 2021 DGIQ Conference (Data Governance Information Quality), she shared her ideas about strategy and described how she was applying Alex Osterwalder's Business Model Canvas to data. I was intrigued. As someone who preaches the need for a strategy to prioritize what is important to your organization and guide your data management journey, I wanted to know more. Marilu had developed her own data strategy method and was considering writing a book. I immediately encouraged her. I was sure she had something unique to share and that her approach would add significantly to the field of data management.

My initial instincts were right. Our data community needs this book – and by extension, those we serve need this book. With the "what", the "why", and the "how" outlined here, you will be well equipped to use data strategy to help your organization be more successful.

As a final note, let us celebrate the fact that this is one of the first data management books by a woman out of Latin America. Who better than Marilu to bring this message forward and share it with the world?

Are you ready? Turn the page and get to work!

Danette McGilvray
President, Granite Falls Consulting, Inc.
Consultant, Trainer, Speaker, Coach.
Author of *Executing Data Quality Projects: Ten Steps to Quality Data and Trusted Information™*,
2ⁿᵈ Ed. (2021, Elsevier/Academic Press)

Introduction

Most books with "Data Strategy" in their titles focus on strategies for Data Analytics and Big Data.[1] Reviewing the outline of the available books in the market, I noticed the typical pattern is to talk about Data Strategy from a philosophical point of view, describing **WHAT** it is and **WHY** it is essential. Some books talk about how to execute a Data Strategy, but no book I have found presents a step-by-step and artifact-supported method on **HOW** to define Data Strategies, which is what this book will do. This book will present **The Data Strategy PAC Method** (Pragmatic, Agile, and Communicable - *in the sense of readily communicated*). I presented this method at a high level in international forums like Dataversity EDW 2021, DGIQ 2021, EDW Digital 2022, and EDW Digital 2023, with excellent and positive feedback from attendees. Now I want to share that methodology in detail with the wider Data Management community.

The Data Strategy PAC Method focuses on three interdependent concepts:

- **Data Strategy** is the highest-level guidance available to an organization, focusing data-related activities on articulated **data goal achievements** and providing direction and specific guidance when faced with a stream of decisions or uncertainties. (Aiken & Harbour, 2017)

- **Data Management** is the development, execution, and supervision of plans, policies, programs, and practices that deliver, control, protect, and enhance the value of data and information assets throughout their lifecycles. (DAMA International, 2017)

- **Data Governance** is the exercise of authority, control, and shared decision-making (planning, monitoring, and enforcement) over the management of data assets. (DAMA International, 2017)

The Data Management Building (Figure 1) depicts how these concepts relate to each other. The building represents an organization. Data Management, with all its functions surrounded by the core function, Data Governance, represents the foundation of the building. The apartments on each floor of the building represent the organizational units. The grounded building is due to the robustness of the foundation complemented by the extensions of Data Governance through Data Stewards living on each floor and Data Policies to be followed by the inhabitants of each

---

[1] Modern Data Strategy (Fleckenstein, 2018); Data Strategy and the Enterprise Data Executive (Aiken & Harbour, 2017); Data Strategy: from definition to Execution (Wallis, 2021); Data Strategy: How to Profit from a World of Big Data, Analytics, and the Internet of Things (Marr, 2021); Driving Data Strategy: The Ultimate Data Marketing Strategy to Rocket Your Global Business (Fawzi, 2021); AI and Data Strategy: Harnessing the business potential of Artificial Intelligence and Big Data (Marshall, 2019); Data Strategy (Adelman, 2005); Data Strategy Canvas for Healthcare Organizations (Walters, 2019).

apartment. Four pillars complement the building structure to prevent collapse: the Data Governance Operating Model, the Data Architecture Operating Model, the Metadata Management Operating Model, and the Data Quality Operating Model.

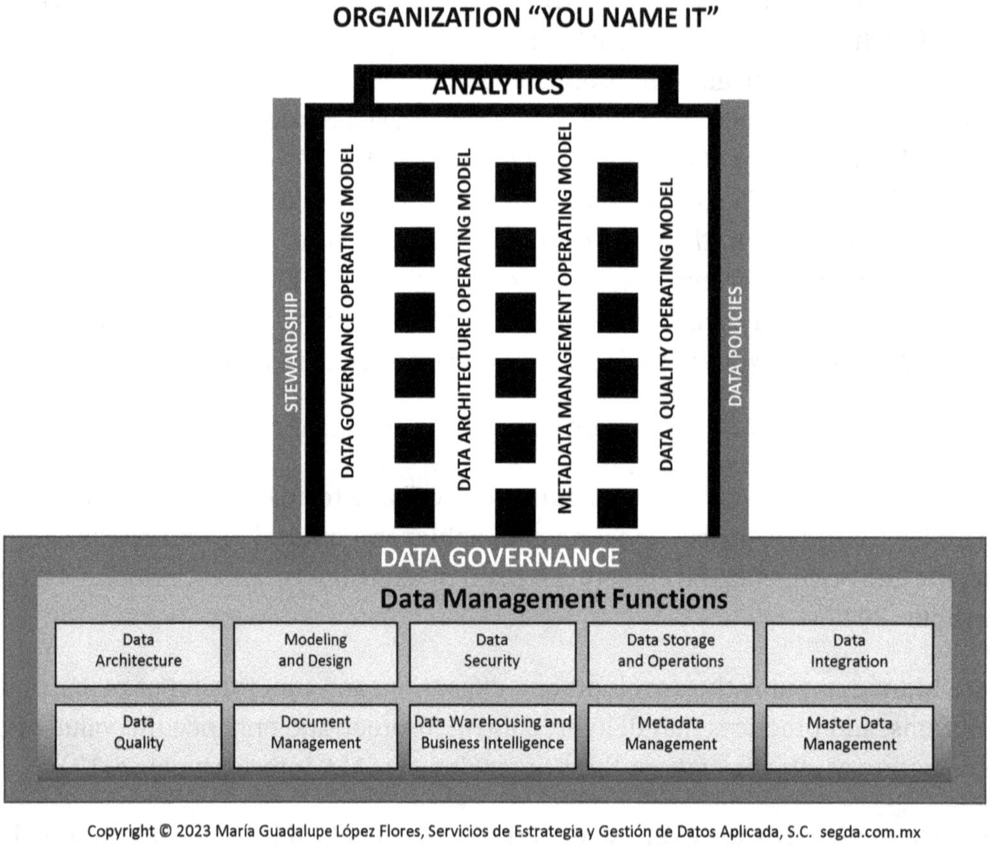

ORGANIZATION "YOU NAME IT"

Figure 1 The Data Management Building Metaphor

Based on the Data Strategies Framework (see Figures 2 and 3), Data Strategy is the master guide to constructing the building from the foundation to the roof. The Data Strategies canvases are the blueprints to communicate this to the construction workers. The Data Leader (e.g., Chief Data Officer, Data Governance Lead) is the construction site manager. Through the pages of this book, you will find detailed explanations of the Data Strategies Framework, the canvases used to document Data Strategies, and the specific steps to follow to create a continuous process to produce and maintain the Data Strategies.

I dedicated half of my 32-year corporate life in the financial sector to Data Management-related topics. During those years, I faced different Data Strategies. I did not know what to include in a Data Strategy, but I could tell that they were incomplete and not wholly aligned with business priorities. When I "retired" in 2019, I wanted to keep my mind active, so I started my journey as a Data Management consultant and trainer. My first assignment was defining a Data Strategy. I had no idea how to do it, so I searched the Internet for specific methods. I did not find exactly what I wanted, but I was inspired to develop new ideas.

One source of Data Strategy inspiration was Global Data Strategy, Ltd.´s (GDS) Framework, inspired by Donna Burbank.[2] From it, I learned how to relate Data Strategy with Enterprise Strategy.

In addition, DAMA (Data Management Association)[3] is an inspiration for me. DAMA is a not-for-profit, vendor- and technology-neutral professional organization which has developed a comprehensive Data Management Framework that has guided me since 2012.[4] (See the *DMBoK 2nd Edition* (2017).[5]) I got deeply involved with it when I coordinated and edited its translation to Spanish. I learned about this organization while trying to educate myself to understand how to create a Data Governance practice, and a long relationship with DAMA began.

Another source of inspiration was DCAM, the Data Management Capability Assessment Model Guide 2.2 (**Enterprise Data Management Council, 2021**).[6] My involvement as one of the translators of the Spanish edition allowed me to get a deep understanding of it.

Still, the most potent source of inspiration was Alex Osterwalder's *Business Model Canvas.*[7] I was introduced to Osterwalder's approach in 2006 during an Enterprise Architecture Course I designed with a University in Mexico, and I have used it ever since. Emulating an artist's use of canvas, Osterwalder depicts on a single slide all that is needed to understand, at first glance, the Business Model of any organization, regardless of its size and the sector it belongs to. If a canvas can successfully document Business Models, why shouldn't it be a powerful tool for writing Data Strategies?

These sources inspired me to design a method for writing Data Strategies using canvases that clearly show, each in a single slide, what to do, what organizational structure to use, what type of data to include, what initiatives to involve, and what metrics to display to show progress and effectiveness. **The Data Strategy PAC Method** comprises three components: a framework, a set of canvases, and a strategy cycle (Figure 2).

- **The Data Strategies Framework** is the first component of **The Data Strategy PAC Method** (Figure 3). It accommodates the idea that there is not a single Data Strategy but

---

[2] Global Data Strategy, Ltd.´s (GDS) Framework https://globaldatastrategy.com/

[3] Data Management Association International https://www.dama.org

[4] DAMA's Framework https://www.dama.org/cpages/dmbok-2-wheel-images

[5] DAMA DMBoK 2nd Edition https://technicspub.com/dmbok/

[6] Enterprise Data Management Council -DCAM Framework https://edmcouncil.org/frameworks/dcam/

[7] Alexander Osterwalder https://www.alexosterwalder.com/ Business Model Canvas https://bit.ly/3LSV4bb

several. The Framework shows the different Data Strategies and their relationships to other organizational strategies. We review this Framework in Chapter 3.

- Corporate life taught me how hard it is to engage stakeholders. Attracting their attention and getting buy-in requires a pragmatic, agile, and clear approach. This is why I developed the second component, **The Set of Data Strategy Canvases**, to describe each type of Data Strategy (Figure 4). We explore these canvases in Chapter 5.

- The third component, **The Data Strategy Cycle**, is a set of ten steps to follow annually to keep the strategies aligned (Figure 5). We cover this cycle in Chapter 7.

I have applied this method in several organizations from different sectors since 2019. I founded SEGDA (Spanish acronym for Strategy and Applied Data Management Services), a consultancy company based in Mexico but remotely serving organizations in different locations. SEGDA is focused on helping organizations define their Data Strategies and implement Data Management Operating Models. The practice of these real-life cases has enabled me to refine the methodology.

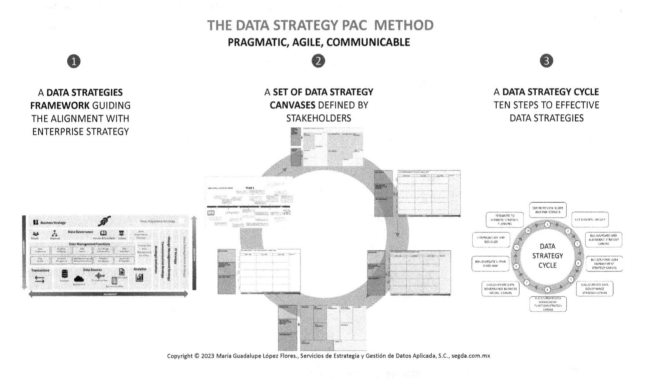

Figure 2 Components of The Data Strategy PAC Method

In 2021, 2022, and 2023, I presented **The Data Strategy PAC Method** at Enterprise Data World (EDW). Due to the COVID-19 pandemic, these three conferences were digital, but the feedback I received from attendees was very positive. Data Governance and Information Quality (DGIQ) 2021 was an in-person conference in San Diego, where I could see the audience's positive reaction from the standing-room-only crowd. The comments I received after EDW 2022 Digital were fuel for me, letting me know I was on the right path. I knew it was worth converting the story I managed to tell in 40 minutes into a book with enough detail to let you know how to use the method but without the burden of a long theoretical work. I hope you find it helpful.

A **DATA STRATEGIES FRAMEWORK** GUIDING THE ALIGNMENT WITH ENTERPRISE STRATEGY

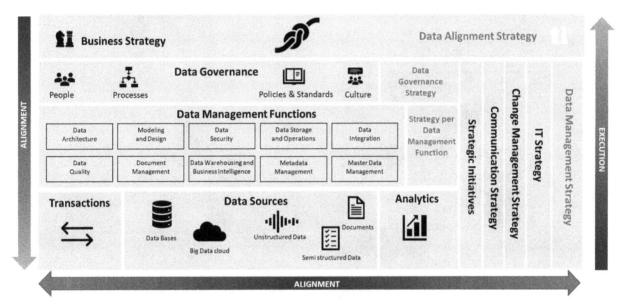

Figure 3 Component 1: The Data Strategies Framework

Based on what I saw and heard in the organizations I worked with and the feedback from people I trained in Data Management, I noticed that Data Strategies aligning data efforts to business strategic objectives were tough to find. There is not a widespread awareness among the CxOs about the relevance of having a Data Strategy aligned with business objectives. And most organizations do not treat data as the strategic enterprise asset it should be.

Since 2017, I have met some gurus in this fantastic journey of Data Management. I have even had the good fortune to befriend some of them. I thought readers would be interested to see what these experts think about the role of Data Strategy in enabling successful data governance, so I asked them. I am honored to have had the opportunity to interview Bill Inmon, Melanie Mecca, James Price, Håkan Edvinsson, Tom Redman, David Plotkin, and Danette McGilvray. You will find one interview at the end of each chapter in this book.

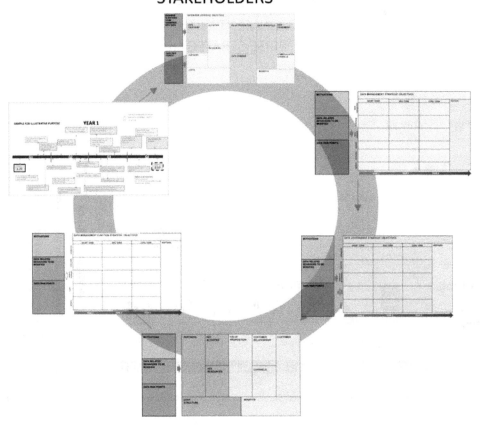

Figure 4 Component 2: The Set of Data Strategy Canvases

A **DATA STRATEGY CYCLE**
TEN STEPS TO EFFECTIVE
DATA STRATEGIES

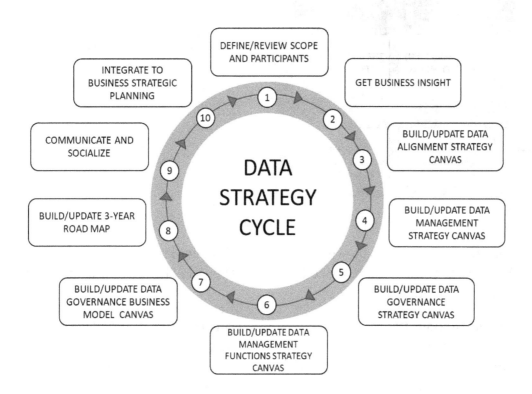

Figure 5 Component 3: The Data Strategy Cycle

How to Use This Book

This book is divided into two parts (Figure 6):

- Part 1 provides the context to understand the concepts and rationale behind **The Data Strategy PAC Method.** It describes Component 1, The Data Strategies Framework, and Component 2, The Set of Data Strategy Canvases.

- Part 2 describes Component 3 of **The Data Strategy PAC Method**, The Data Strategy Cycle, which focuses on implementing the methodology.

You may want to skip Part 1 and go straight to the Data Strategy Cycle, but I strongly recommend going through Part 1 to understand the motivations and support for each cycle's steps. Besides, in each of the Part 1 chapters, you will get specific learning and takeaway points. I designed the chapters to tell a coherent story if you go through them sequentially.

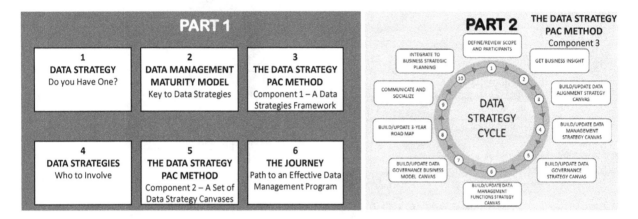

Figure 6 Book Map

At the beginning of each chapter, you will find the Book Map indicating where you are in your journey. In Part 2, each of the steps described will have The Data Strategy Cycle Map indicating where you are in each of the steps in the cycle.

Capitalization Convention: I have capitalized all the terms relevant to the ideas presented in this book to remark on their importance in the **Data Management** (this is the first example of this convention) practice. When individual terms are used (data, management, strategy), I do not capitalize them. I have also capitalized the buzzwords closely related to the topics addressed in this work.

This book has a website companion. There you will find templates for the artifacts mentioned in this book, examples of the Data Strategy Canvases, study cases, and other references you may find helpful. This is also the place where you will be able to drop your comments and share your experience using this method. Please take the opportunity to try the method and tell us how your experience was.

The Context

Even though this book does not pretend to be a treatise on Data Strategy or Data Management (yes, capitalized due to the relevance of these two concepts), I need to level set and establish a context before describing the methodology itself.

Part 1 will present this context in Chapters 1 - 6, starting with the more general topics and moving to the core components used in the method.

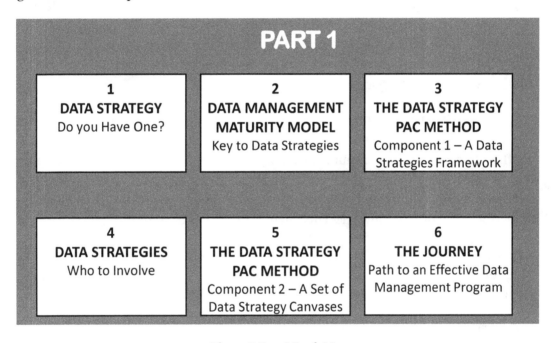

Figure 7 Part 1 Book Map

- **Chapter 1: Data Strategy: Do You Have One?** The opening chapter sets the stage for **The Data Strategy PAC Method.** It presents several definitions of strategy that inspired the method described in this book and level sets on the definition of Data Strategy used here. This chapter explores the perceived maturity of the organizations on Data Strategy by referring to existing studies, including one conducted by the author in collaboration with a University in Mexico, to understand the current state of Data Management and its relation to Data Strategy in Latin America.

- **Chapter 2: Data Management Maturity Model: Key to Data Strategies.** The main purpose of Data Strategies is to move the organization from its current state to a desired one. A crucial question is what the desired state is. Here's where using a Data

Management Maturity Model is core to understanding what capabilities are in place and which must be put in place. This chapter addresses the relevance of capability-based Data Management Maturity Models and their role in guiding Data Strategies.

- **Chapter 3: The Data Strategy PAC Method: Component 1 – The Data Strategies Framework.** One of this book's essential messages is that Data Strategy is not a concept in the singular but in the plural. This chapter describes the different Data Strategies that must be developed for an organization to get more value from its data. It also describes how these strategies relate to each other and other Business and IT strategies in the organization.

- **Chapter 4: Data Strategies: Who to Involve.** The role of the Data Governance Lead has evolved over the last few years. The responsibility of this role goes beyond defining Data Governance policies, setting data standards, and solving or escalating data issues. The current Data Governance Lead is very active in promoting data culture and ensuring Data Strategies are effective. The Data Governance Lead must orchestrate the participation of key stakeholders across the organization. This chapter describes how to do this without dying trying.

- **Chapter 5: The Data Strategy PAC Method: Component 2 – A Set of Data Strategy Canvases.** In 2005, Alexander Osterwalder defined the Business Model Canvas as a method to capture and communicate an organization's business model on a single slide. This approach has been a fundamental source of inspiration for The Data Strategy PAC Method, which proposes a canvas specifically designed for each of the Data Strategies in the Data Strategies Framework. This chapter describes each of these canvases.

- **Chapter 6: The Journey: Path to an Effective Data Management Program.** This chapter explains the path to an effective Data Management Program, beginning with a common question asked by people involved with this work: Where do we start?

At the end of each chapter, you will find three closing items:

Key Concepts

Three Things to Keep in Mind

An Interview on Data Strategy

1. Data Strategy: Do You Have One?

The essence of strategy is choosing what not to do.

Michael Porter

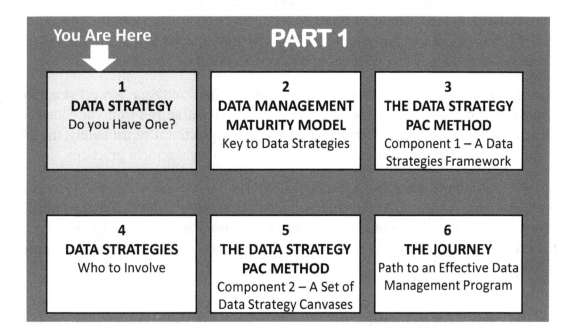

1.1. The Role of Data Management in the Digital Transformation Era

In 2012, I got deeply involved in Data Management when management asked me to create the first Data Governance Office in the organization where I dedicated 32 years of my professional life. Because of the 2008 financial crisis, I had the opportunity to start my journey in Data Management after several years of trying to promote Enterprise Architecture discipline and implementing Architecture Governance.[8] To be better prepared for implementing the Data Governance practice, I attended the EDW (Enterprise Data World) Conference for the

---

[8] Financial crisis of 2007-2008 https://bit.ly/3yUEkNK; 2008 Financial Crisis https://bit.ly/3ySiiva; The Collapse of Lehman Brothers: A Case Study https://bit.ly/3NBEy0F

first time, where I learned about DAMA International. Since then, I have dedicated a significant amount of time as a volunteer evangelizing the importance of Data Management.

Convinced that this is a continuous journey where we never stop learning, I regularly attend data-related events. Speakers often remark on the explosive growth of data in recent years. In my early presentations, I quoted statistics stating that IDC[9] estimated the data growth globally for 2020 at 44 ZB (zettabytes). In March 2021, IDC published its annual DataSphere and StorageSphere[10] forecasts, measuring the amount of data created, consumed, and stored annually. By 2020, 64.2 ZB were created, 45% more than expected in their previous prediction in 2019. The COVID-19 pandemic caused this unpredicted increase, which resulted in more people working, learning, and entertaining themselves remotely and buying goods online, according to Dave Reinsel, senior vice president of IDC's GlobalDataSphere. This report also indicates that less than 2% of this new data was saved and retained into 2021. The reflection is that producing or collecting vast volumes of data is useless unless we can use it.

From inception, we must have transparent processes to understand data, protect sensitive data, and ensure data is of good quality. This is the only way to tell real stories from the collected data. We can achieve all these through formal Data Management practice. Unfortunately, the increase in data contrasts with the slow pace at which we adopt Data Management practices.

In 2017, The Economist published an article titled "The world's most valuable resource is no longer oil, but data," which made the catchphrase "Data is the new Oil" familiar to us all. Since then, many articles and discussions have tried to define whether data is really the new oil and whether it is worth comparing data with oil, which is non-renewable, while data keeps growing.

Many say that data is a strategic enterprise asset, but it is not always treated as such in real life practice. Reasons why we don't treat data as a strategic asset are very clearly captured in *The Leader's Data Manifesto* (Manifesto, 2016),[11] a must-read for all leaders in the organizations, including data leaders, to digest and discuss it with their teams to understand the data's relevance.

Two buzzwords have invaded conferences and specialized professional networks in the last years, *Digital Transformation* and *Data Driven*. But these are not new concepts at all. Digital Transformation started in the late 1990s, when process automation started and the use of the Internet expanded.[12] We can find references to Data Driven (activities or decisions supported by data rather than intuition) over the last 15 years. We can see the term applied to learning or

---

[9] International Data Corporation https://www.idc.com/

[10] Worldwide Global DataSphere Forecast, 2021-2025 https://bit.ly/3sWyVlH

[11] https://dataleaders.org

[12] Digital Transformation History https://bit.ly/3cww7q8

any specific process when it is driven by data. But over recent years, most organizations have made it a goal to become Data Driven, meaning they try to use data to power decision-making and other related activities efficiently, in real-time.[13]

As for Digital Transformation, which the COVID-19 pandemic accelerated, there is still no complete understanding of what it means. We can look at a primary definition, *"Digital Transformation* is the adoption of digital technology by a company. Common goals for its implementation are to improve efficiency, value, or innovation" (Wikipedia, 2022). A more helpful definition comes from TechTarget: *"Digital transformation* is the incorporation of computer-based technologies into an organization's products, processes, and strategies. Organizations undertake digital transformation to engage better and serve their workforce and customers and thus improve their ability to compete" (TechTarget, 2022). However, Digital Transformation is more than just adopting new digital technology to sell products or services online. It also involves adjusting the business model, internal processes, and organizational culture. Moreover, beneath this, we must manage a vast amount of data appropriately to have a successful Digital Transformation. Therefore, I see Data Management as the foundation for any Digital Transformation initiative to succeed.

During a Data Management 101 class I facilitated, a student told me that he saw Data Management as the foundation of a building. That analogy made sense because of my Enterprise Architecture perspective and what it takes to construct a building. Laying the foundation is among the most expensive phases of the construction process. However, the foundation is not perceived when the building is complete because it is covered. People usually admire a building's façade, its design and functionality, and how intelligent it is. I live in Mexico City, a seismic zone whipped by severe earthquakes. I have witnessed how new and modern buildings have collapsed for not having proper foundations. Well, the same thing happens with Data Management. It is expensive, and it does not show off. Data Management disciplines do not shine, but they can make the difference between an organization growing healthy and one struggling to survive and eventually disappearing.

The uncertainty of the economy and the unexpected changes in consumer behaviors have been important motivations for organizations to include in their strategic objectives to become Data Driven organizations. Data scientists work on information models to provide insight into the organization and predict customers' behaviors about the products or services offered. Data Management's functions seem far from the fancy and sexy jobs young people seek around Data Science. They want to analyze data using innovative algorithms and leading-edge tools like AI (Artificial Intelligence) and ML (Machine Learning). However, those tools and algorithms cannot do their work unless they have reliable data. Helping make data reliable is the work of Data Management. Poorly managed data is risky and costly, even if those costs are largely hidden. Keeping a Data Management program alive can be expensive, but not having it can lead the

---

[13] What is Data Driven https://bit.ly/3cFtKB9

organization to collapse. Thus, analytics, as related to data consumption, depends on the quality of the data supplied.

Every day, more organizations are willing to step up on advanced analytics to get value from having data. Sometimes though, they do not know the questions they want to answer. A statement spread worldwide in the last years is that data scientists spend over 80% of their time doing data gathering and cleansing instead of working on the design and training of information models, applying the magic of their algorithms.[14] The fact is that they spend a lot of time and effort finding, cleaning, and understanding data due to the lack of Metadata.

A few weeks ago, when chatting with my nephew doing a Data Science bachelor's degree, I was surprised to hear they have a data quality course in their program. At first, I felt glad, but then I realized the University was normalizing that data scientists must deal with cleaning data instead of creating programs to prepare Data Management professionals. The relevant idea here is that for data scientists to do their work and tell true stories, organizations must formally adopt all Data Management disciplines to gather, produce, preserve, document, secure, and provide data that fits the purpose of the different stakeholders in the organization. That's why Data Management is the foundation for successful Digital Transformation and Data Driven initiatives.

BARC's November 2018 survey on Data Monetization showed that 40% of the 200 surveyed organizations were running a data monetization project or had already begun to monetize data through improving internal processes.[15] This contrasted with only 6% of the organizations referring to monetizing data by creating new lines of business. But the most revealing part of this study was that 56% of respondents said a lack of data quality was a constant challenge when pursuing data monetization. And here is again the point that links data consumption with the effective practice of Data Management.

1.2.   How do Organizations Perceive Data Strategy?

Data Strategy is gaining its own space in the data world. We can find several articles and books related to this concept. Even international conference events like EDW and DGIQ include a track dedicated to Data Strategy. Most of the literature on Data Strategy deals with the explanation of **WHAT** it is, while others include **WHY** it is so important to have one. Still, very little ink and

---

[14] I found an interesting article analyzing all the different studies on this matter, stating that data scientists don't spend as much as 80% of their time cleaning data. Perhaps there is a data quality problem related to measuring this concept? Do data scientists spend 80% of their time cleaning data? Turns out, no? https://bit.ly/3lJBF1H

[15] Business Application Research Center https://barc-research.com/ . BARC Survey Finds Data Monetization Is in The Early Stages of Adoption But Is Expanding https://bit.ly/3LMyCAv/

very few keystrokes help explain **HOW** to produce a Data Strategy that addresses business needs in a prioritized way.

While preparing for my participation at DGIQ 2021, I searched for statistics on how organizations were doing Data Strategies. While I didn't find exactly what I was looking for, I found an interesting study by BARC on the impact of data silos.[16] In response to questions about the cultural and organizational challenges that influence the existence of information silos, 42% of the respondents said that lack of communication was the most critical challenge to solve to reduce data silos, and 30% said it was the lack of Data Strategy.

Most Data Management studies include only European, Asia Pacific, or North American (Canada and US) organizations. Few attempt to understand how Latin American organizations adopt Data Management. That is why when asked to participate with a university in Mexico, UPAEP (Universidad Popular Autonoma del Estado de Puebla), in designing and implementing a study on the current state of Data Management in Latin America, I happily agreed. I proposed expanding the scope to research how Data Management was related to Data Strategy. The findings of this research will be presented at the end of this chapter.

Even before getting hard data about Latin America, I built an image of what was going on with Data Management and Data Strategy in the region.

Interest in Data Management has been increasing in the last few years. Most organizations pay more attention to data because they work in regulated sectors (finance, insurance, health) or have had bad experiences with poor-quality data. They are hiring people for data-specific roles and investing vast amounts of money in leading-edge technologies and professional services. They are implementing data lakes and MDM (Master Data Management) platforms and adopting AI (Artificial Intelligence) to make data "speak" and tell stories.

As a consultant, I talk extensively with people who lead Data Governance programs. When I bring up the importance of Data Strategy, I hear two common responses: "Oh, we already have a Data Strategy," or "I am working on it; that is why they hired me." Digging deeper, I usually find that organizations do not have a Data Strategy, at least not a holistic and effective one. A Data Strategy is holistic when it covers the entire organization's needs and accounts for requirements from each organizational unit. An effective strategy requires engaging representatives of the organization in its definition. If they are not involved, the strategy may have features that make it less effective. Data Management practitioners have shared with me common characteristics of ineffective strategies. For example:

---

[16] BARC: Infografics – "DATA Black Holes" https://bit.ly/3sWK5qm

- **Technical Orientation:** Organizations with Data Strategy documents, including architectural diagrams, that are technology-oriented and focused on moving to data-related platforms.

- **Lack of Alignment with Business Goals:** Organizations with documented strategies for acquiring, ingesting, and consuming Big Data but not aligned with core business needs and priorities.

- **Lack of Attention to Source Data:** Organizations where data interest is centered on adopting Advanced Analytics platforms to produce predictive information models without clearly defining data domains, sources, and priorities.

- **No Plan for Improvement:** Data Governance leads report they do not need more assessments, as they have already gone through several, but they still do not use a Data Management maturity model to guide their data-related actions.

- **The Technical Design does not Account for Business Goals**: Organizations aiming to be Data Warehouse-centric do not understand why their data repository is not widely used when it comes out that its design does not meet business strategic objectives.

- **Lack of Knowledge of Business Strategy**: Not even Business Strategy is known.

  - No written Data Strategy is in place, but a Customer MDM (Master Data Management) project is ongoing because other organizations in the sector are doing that. Still, no customer duplication pain exists.
  - Organizations with high efficiency in Metadata Management, but data leads do not know what to do next.
  - Organizations living the third or fourth attempt to implement Data Governance, after failed experiences, and censoring specific terms: *"Please don't mention stewardship."*

- **Data Strategy Exists but is not Used:** Organizations where, if a Data Strategy exists, it is not used to guide and prioritize the data-related actions or manage the expectations for Data Management across the organization.

Does any of this sound familiar to you? Look inside your organization at this moment. Do you have a Data Strategy in place? Is it accessible to everybody in the organization that might be interested? Is it easy to read and understand? Is it used to guide action and manage expectations on Data Management? Is it a live document that gets updated when required? Do key stakeholders across the organization define it? Is it considered part of the enterprise's annual business strategic planning? If your answer was positive to all these questions, congratulations! Your organization is one of those rare cases, and you may want to quit reading here. However, if you answered "No" to at least one question, you may find it worthwhile to continue reading. And you will not be alone. A 2021 executive survey by New Vantage Partners, where data-intensive industries were heavily represented, showed that only 30% of the blue-chip organizations expressed they had an articulated Data Strategy.[17]

I based the research that I proposed to UPAEP University on the following problem statement and hypothesis:

Despite the existence of various Data Management frameworks and the growing awareness in companies that they must adopt a formal practice for the management and care of their data, generally expressed as a practice of Data Governance, it seems that a level of maturity has not been reached such that the expected value of the so-called 'strategic asset' can truly be obtained. The references to exploratory studies in this area usually focus on the European and Anglo-Saxon markets, leaving aside the reality in Latin America. It is increasingly common to hear companies expressing frustration about ineffective data governance practices when they invest in technological platforms proposed as the panacea for managing and exploiting data. Yet, they do not obtain the expected benefit.

Hypothesis: The lack of a comprehensive Data Strategy is an obstacle to achieving effective results in implementing Data Management.

The study was entitled *"Situación de la Gestión de Datos y su Vinculación con la Estrategia de Datos en América Latina"* (Current State of Data Management and its Relationship with the Data Strategy in Latin America). The research was collaborative between UPAEP University and SEGDA, a consultancy firm focused on Data Strategy and Data Management Operating Models.[18]

First executed in 2022, the study to track how Data Management maturity is perceived in Latin America will be repeated annually. Of course, this first-ever study on Data Strategy and Data Management in Latin America will interest the countries in this region. Those in other parts of the world, particularly organizations with business units in several countries, and more importantly, those with current or expected business in this region, will also benefit from findings that can guide their Data Strategies. Below is the executive summary of the findings:

- This first year had a good level of penetration with 126 responses, with predominant responses from Mexico (40%), Colombia (14%), Argentina (8%), Chile (8%), Peru (8%), and Ecuador (7%). The remaining 15% was comprised of 7 countries.

- The sectors most present in the responses were Financial (25%), Government (17%), and Information Technology (12%), followed by Education, Consulting, Insurance, Telecommunications, Retail, Energy, and Agro-industrial.

---

[17] 10 Reasons Why Your Organization Still Isn't Data Driven https://bit.ly/3wScRcT

[18] Situación de la Gestión de Datos y su vinculación con la Estrategia de Datos en América Latina https://bit.ly/3oM7Fnt

- Respondents were mainly Managers of areas focused on data (31%), followed by IT Managers (13%) and Business areas (11%). Only 10% of respondents had a C-level position in their organization.

Table 1 Latin America Research Findings on Data Management and Data Strategy

Latin America Research Findings		
Data Strategy	To what degree is Data Strategy developed and used in organizations?	The largest group of respondents (46%) reported that their Data Strategy is in development. This number speaks to a significant interest in this topic, as well as awareness of its relevance. Of these, 12% indicate that alignment with the business is contemplated, but only 9% say the Data Strategy is used to prioritize the Data Management activities, and 8% report Data Strategy is used to prioritize Data Governance development. 32% of respondents indicated their organization had an approved Data Strategy.
Frameworks	How well are existing resources known?	The results clearly show that DAMA's framework is the most widely known in the region (55%), followed by DCAM at 22%, and DMM (Data Management Maturity Model[19]) at 11%. It is interesting to note that 13% reported not being familiar with any Data Management framework, which shows that there is still a lot of evangelizing to be done.
Obstacles to Effective Data Governance	Which is the main obstacle when implementing Data Governance?	Many respondents recognized the need for Data Governance to help solve data-related problems. There is a widespread belief that it is difficult to convince senior management to invest in Data Governance efforts. However, only 12% of respondents refer to an unconvinced Senior Management as an obstacle to implementing Data Governance; 31% say that the main block is a lack of understanding of Data Governance, and 20% indicate that the main obstacle is the lack of a clear and comprehensive Data Strategy.

---

[19] Data Management Maturity Model Introduction https://bit.ly/3coOX2t

Latin America Research Findings		
Data Management Maturity	What level of maturity is perceived?	Most organizations start building their Data Management Disciplines one at a time. Often, they are motivated by regulatory pressures and the need to be able to exchange information. This is why Security, Storage, and Data Architecture are often more mature than the other disciplines. However, there is an awareness of the need to articulate all disciplines, confirmed by the level of perceived maturity of Data Governance, which is the fourth highest. What is surprising is that Data Quality is in eighth place of priority and Metadata in ninth place since both are necessary for a better and more agile understanding of the data.
Data Culture	How widespread is the understanding of Data Management?	44% of respondents recognize significant efforts to disseminate the importance of data and its proper management in their organizations. However, only 8% indicate they have a common language to describe Data Management and its relevance. The latter reinforces that 31% say that the main obstacle to successfully implementing Data Governance is a lack of knowledge about Data Governance. This tells us that there is still a need in the Latin America Region to strengthen educational programs in Data Management.
Data Analytics	How linked is it to Data Management?	32% of respondents said they recognized an established practice of Analytics in their organizations. However, only 10% indicated that the practice was fully implemented and operating for the entire organization (an indicator of a data-oriented organization). 50% of the latter population said they had evidence of the contribution information models made to the fulfillment of strategic objectives. Notably, 31% of respondents reported a link between Data Management and Data Analytics in their organizations. In 8% of cases, both practices are led by the same person.

The respondents were very generous in answering two open questions about the perceived impact of the Data Strategy and the benefits of a Data Strategy in cases where the Data Management practice was partially or fully implemented.

The balance indicates a strong awareness of the benefits of having a Data Strategy against the multiple negative impacts of not having one. For example, high costs associated with isolated or duplicated efforts and investment in underutilized technological platforms.

The results for Latin America are very similar to those reported by New Vantage Partners in their 2021 executive survey, at least on the existence of Data Strategy (32% in Latin America vs. 30% in New Vantage Partners' studio). When asked about the main obstacle to implementing effective Data Governance, 30% said it was the lack of understanding of both Data Governance and Data Strategy (meaning more training is required). The lack of a Data Strategy was the main obstacle reported by 20% of the respondents. These results imply that people working in Data Management and Data Governance will benefit from learning to formulate and use Data Strategies.

1.3.   A Good Starting Point: What is a Strategy?

Let's begin with a definition: What is a strategy? I would say it's what you need to win a game. One of my best childhood memories is playing tic tac toe with my father. I liked it, but it was very frustrating for me not to be able to win. Then my father taught me a strategy that made a difference. I now realize that anyone can play a game just by knowing the rules, but winning requires strategy, practice, and discipline.

My first project as a consultant was at a large and well-established entertainment company. They had worked with different consultancies to define a sound Data Strategy, but were not satisfied with the outcome. So my first assignment was to help them define their Data Strategy. At that point, I could tell if something I saw was not a Data Strategy, but I did not know what an effective Data Strategy should look like, so I started researching. I found some books and articles with interesting titles that told me what a Data Strategy is and why it is important to have one, but I needed something to help me produce it.

Although the term *strategy* has a military origin, its application has expanded over time. In the mid-1960s, it was first applied to business by Igor Ansoff.[20] The Cambridge Dictionary says *strategy* is "a detailed plan for achieving success in situations such as war, politics, business, industry, or sport, or the skill of planning for such situations." According to DAMA, *strategy* is

---

[20] Igor Ansoff Russian-American mathematician coined the term "strategy" for business. https://bit.ly/3yXtlDe

"A set of decisions that set a direction and define an approach to solving a problem or achieving a goal" (DAMA International, 2010).

However, I do not intend to present definitions you can find yourself. Instead, I'll focus on those that caught my attention and which set the context for Part 2 of this book, the Data Strategy Cycle, as the component of **The Data Strategy PAC Method** dedicated to implementation.

The first definition that caught my attention was by Rich Horwath: "Strategy is not Aspiration. Strategy is not the Best Practice. Strategy is the **intelligent allocation of resources** through a unique system of activities to achieve a goal."[21] This definition applies to the data world. I have seen Data Strategies that describe the desired end state or the industry's best practices and standards to be adopted. Still, if these don't prioritize what to do or account for the people assigned to get to the desired state, they are not really strategies.

Peter Aiken and Todd Harbour propose an excellent definition: "Strategy is the **highest-level guidance** available to an organization, focusing activities on **articulated goal achievement** and providing direction and specific guidance when faced with a stream of decisions or uncertainties." This concept translates naturally into a definition of **Data Strategy**: Data Strategy is the highest-level guidance available to an organization, focusing data-related activities on articulated **data goal achievements** and providing direction and specific guidance when faced with a stream of decisions or uncertainties" (Aiken & Harbour, 2017).

Donna Burbank, a recognized data strategist, states, "A Data Strategy requires an **understanding of the data needs inherent in the Business Strategy**" (DATAVERSITY, 2021).[22] This insight reveals where we should start when defining a Data Strategy: first know the business strategy. Although this may sound obvious, the business strategy is not published or widely known in many organizations. It does not mean, though, that it does not exist. Every organization has a strategy, no matter how basic it is. However, sometimes, it exists only within one person's mind or a limited number of persons' minds. Understanding the business needs in data is essential to defining a Data Strategy. Expressing those needs is not easy, and neither is creating consensus on the requirements and how to prioritize them.

Ian Wallis discusses the difference between defensive and offensive Data Strategy. For example, many organizations start with a defensive view to meet compliance requirements. As they mature their Data Management practices, some can move to an offensive position, making Data Management part of business as usual. This change positions them to get value from their data (Wallis, 2021).

---

[21] Strategic Thinking Institute https://www.strategyskills.com/what-is-strategy/

[22] https://www.linkedin.com/in/donnaburbank/ Global Data Strategy https://globaldatastrategy.com/

In a May 2022 interview, Data Management guru Bill Inmon shared his understanding of the relationship between strategy and Data Architecture (see the end of this chapter for the complete interview):

"Suppose you are on a ship. You are in the middle of the Pacific. Strategy tells you that you need to direct the ship meaningfully. Otherwise, you will never get to where you are going.

Data Architecture is like a compass or a map. With Data Architecture, you know where you are heading to.

You need BOTH strategy – piloting the ship – and the map and compass to tell you what the right heading is. Without a map, you don't know where you are going."

When discussing Data Strategies, we first must think horizontally and account for the organization's units (all the lines of business, shared services like finance, legal, compliance, HR, IT, etc.). This horizontal view helps to identify and prioritize business questions, data-related pain points, and motivations. Then we can think vertically when selecting a business unit to work with; we need to identify related business processes, data domains, data sources, and strategic initiatives related. These different views provide a map of the organization and its needs. A Data Strategy offers a tangible way to manage expectations related to Data Management and Data Governance (because many people do not understand these concepts). Data Strategies help describe what to do first, with which organizational units, and with which data, processes, or reports.

Different organizations will define Data Strategies with different scopes. Some focus on adopting new technologies, others on acquiring data. Some account for the whole enterprise, while others focus on a specific organization area. I propose starting with a *Holistic Data Strategy* defined by representatives from across the organization. This group must understand the business and data-related problems in each part of the organization.

A holistic Data Strategy presents a horizontal view of the organization and its data. With this view established, turn to the verticals. Pick a strategic business objective and drill down through the different Data Management functions that support the objective (Data Governance Strategy, Data Quality Strategy, Data Architecture Strategy, IT Strategy, etc.). This produces a set of Data Strategies, each with a specific focus and scope, but all related through their connection to overall business strategy and their common goals. We describe this approach in Chapter 3.

With all the above in mind, I formulated the following definition, which we will use throughout the book:

Data Strategies are the highest-level guidance in an organization on intelligently assigning resources to work in an integrated way to achieve data-related goals and contribute to achieving business strategic objectives.

1.4.   What Should We Expect to Find in a Data Strategy?

When first working on Data Strategy, I researched what a Data Strategy should include. There was no standard agreement. Some publications discussed Data Strategies having five or more core components, with these components related to how to acquire, integrate, secure, store, process, and analyze your data. Others included the tools side of the story and the ownership of data and tools. Some Data Strategy frameworks came from data-related platforms or software tools, making the Data Strategies very technology-oriented. That is why it's not surprising to find this type of strategy in many organizations. Recent work has helped clarify the approach. Peter Aiken and Todd Harbour discuss five critical components of Data Strategy: data vision, data goal, data objectives, supporting strategies, and critical initiatives (Aiken & Harbour, 2017). Ian Wallis asserts that Data Strategy should cover Data Management, including the exploitation of structured and unstructured data (Wallis, 2021). Wallis also considers reporting, analytics, insight, and knowledge management as part of data strategy. Michelle Knight describes the components of a well-developed Data Strategy (Knight, 2021):

- A robust Data Management vision
- A strong business case/reason
- Guiding principles
- Well-considered data goals
- Metrics and measurements of progress and success
- Short-term and long-term objectives
- Suitably designed and understood roles and responsibilities.

This is very similar to what **The Data Strategy PAC Method** considers when building the Data Strategies. A Data Strategy should present at the highest level in the organization the elements that enable all levels in the organization to understand what data is needed to support business objectives, in which order, and who must take action. **The Data Strategy PAC Method** groups the main content of Data Strategies into the following six components:

1. Alignment to Business Strategy
2. Data Required
3. The Rationale for Having a Data Management Program
4. Data Principles
5. Prioritization
     o Data Governance Capabilities
     o Data Management Functions
     o Organization Structure
     o Focus Areas
     o KPIs
6. Partners

1. **Alignment to Business Strategy**: How will data support strategic objectives and Data Management motivations (e.g., having accurate information of business insights and customer behavior)? A good Data Strategy needs to tell the story of what actions to take and in which order to contribute to the fulfillment of business strategic objectives. It usually is hard for people in different parts of the organization to understand why a Data Governance team should exist or why a Metadata Management lead is required, so it is important to have a way to show, for instance, how Metadata Management will support the improvement of data quality and therefore the experience of customers.

2. **Data Required**: A Data Strategy must identify what data is needed to support business objectives and whether this data exists within the organization. For example, the required data to answer those business questions that the executives might ask on a typical workday. Examples include locations of stores with the lowest profitability, which banking products customers with the highest profitability use, experiences that customers have shared on social media, call center demand and wait times, and so on. At the highest level, a Data Strategy will identify and prioritize the data domains or data entities for governance and management. Identifying specific data sets and data elements will come later when working on the Data Management discipline strategy, like in the case of Data Quality.

3. **Rationale**: Why is data needed? How does data contribute to business strategic objectives and data-related pain points? To begin running a Data Management Program or to become a Data Driven organization, we need to identify the fundamental motivations and the benefits of better data handling. Desirable data-related behaviors that need to be expanded across the organization (e.g., people reporting data quality issues, people considering the ethical impact of using sensitive data fields, willingness to share data, etc.) and undesirable behaviors related to data (e.g., not documenting sources used for reports, not documenting Metadata, not using approved data sources, etc.) also need to be described, along with all the problems or pain points regarding data.

4. **Data Principles**: Defining principles to be followed by the organization is a core element of the Data Strategy. As explained by Håkan Edvinsson, failure to define principles often leads to an overreliance on rules, which can cause Data Governance Programs to fail. In his non-coercive approach to Data Governance (Edvinsson H. , 2020), Håkan Edvinsson advocates for governing by principles instead of enforcing rules.

5. **Prioritization**: Since a *strategy* is "an intelligent allocation of resources," a good Data Strategy must prioritize Data Governance capabilities and Data Management functions. High-priority components will be formally adopted and institutionally governed. Not understanding what must be governed first can cause conflict, so prioritizing data-

related actions is critical to the success of the Data Strategy. The main aspects that must be prioritized are the following:

a) **Data Governance Capabilities**: Data Governance is the core function of Data Management. It must orchestrate the other disciplines (e.g., Data Architecture, Data Integration, Data Quality, etc.) and enable organizational capabilities (e.g., set policies, manage a glossary, manage roles, communicate progress, produce KPI dashboards, etc.). The best way to understand the required capabilities is to follow the ones recommended by a formal Data Management Maturity Model (see Chapter 2). These capabilities connect the scope of different Data Strategies (Data Management Strategy, Data Governance Strategy, Data Quality Strategy, etc.), as we will see in Chapters 3 and 5.

b) **Data Management Functions**: Data Management is the foundation of any data-related initiative. Most organizations have some Data Management practices; if they do not, they cannot operate. But these practices are often not formally governed or their governance practices not officially articulated. Therefore, an essential component of a Data Strategy is the formal articulation of required Data Management functions and the priority for addressing them.

c) **Organization Structure**: A primary objective of Data Strategy is to prioritize resource allocation. A critical point in this matter is determining what roles and governing bodies are required to begin the process. An organization launching a Data Management program can start small, with a core Data Governance team comprising a leader, a policies editor, a Metadata Management lead, and a Data Quality analyst. Using an existing governing body to review and discuss data-related matters works better, initially, than setting up numerous councils. Then, as maturity develops, a formal Data Governance Council can be launched as a standing body. We can take a similar approach to data stewardship. Start with a limited part-time group of data stewards the first year; incrementally adding part-time data stewards in different business units. Eventually, move to a full-time group of data stewards or stewardship coordinators as required.

d) **Focus Areas:** Adopting Data Management practices is not a matter of just establishing and developing capabilities. The Data Strategy must clarify the priority of governing different organizational units or lines of business. It must also specify what will be governed (which data entities or domains, reports, processes, etc.). Ideally, these focus areas connect to strategic initiatives that exploit data and contribute to business objectives.

e) **KPIs**: Finally, we need to know how well we are doing and how effectively things work out. For each stage of the Data Strategy and each prioritized component, we need to report progress, through metrics and KPIs, for prioritized Data Management functions. KPIs' scope and complexity change over time, so decisions on what to measure also must be prioritized.

6. **Partners**: When describing the strategy for Data Governance or any other Data Management Functions, it is important to consider how other teams or organizational units can partner with the team executing the strategy. Involving key participants in the definition and execution of the Data Strategies is essential. Their relevance must be explicitly described in each Data Strategy.

1.5.   Key Concepts

Data Strategies are the highest-level guidance in an organization on intelligently assigning resources to work in an integrated way to achieve data-related goals and contribute to achieving business strategic objectives.

1.6.   Things to Keep in Mind

1.   For an organization to have a successful Digital Transformation or Data Driven Transformation, a formal and articulated Data Management practice must be in place.

2.   We can all try to play any game if we have the rules explained, but we can succeed only with a good strategy and continuous training. The same applies to the Data Management game: we need a good strategy and continuous training to succeed as a Data Driven

3.   Data Governance is a core Data Management function in charge of articulating other Data Management functions. The existence of a Data Strategy leads to an effective and successful Data Governance practice.

1.7.   Interview on Data Strategy

EXPERT INTERVIEWED: **Bill Inmon**[23]
Bill Inmon, considered the father of Data Warehousing, is a great data architect, best-selling author with over 30 titles, and founder, Chairman, and CEO of Forest Rim Technology, which has built the world's first Textual ETL software.

---

[23] https://www.linkedin.com/in/billinmon/ https://en.wikipedia.org/wiki/Bill_Inmon

With your vast experience as a Data Intelligence consultant and more recently, in the world of text analysis, how often do you find a well-defined horizontal Data Strategy guiding the data-related work and responding to business strategy in your customers' organizations?

Unfortunately, not very often. Most organizations are led technically by vendors. In some cases, vendors give good advice and good direction. But in most cases, the advice given by the vendor is merely a gimmick to make sales. When a vendor gives advice, you should always ask – whose purposes is the advice given serving? In almost every case, the vendor is merely trying to sell more of whatever the vendor is selling.

What do you think is the role of Data Strategy in the success or failure of a Data Driven Transformation initiative?

Data Strategy to an organization is like the quarterback to the football team. The team isn't going to go far without a good quarterback at the control. There are many aspects and many issues to successfully implement a data architecture. The Data Strategy person needs to be multi-talented and able to handle a diversity of issues. When Data Strategy is coupled with a well-defined data architecture, the organization knows which direction it needs to proceed in.

Data Strategy and a well-defined data architecture are like a ship on the ocean. When a ship does not know what its destination is, any setting of the rudder will do. But when there is a strategy and a data architecture, even in the middle of the Pacific, the organization knows how to set the rudder.

From your perspective, who do you think should drive the creation and maintenance of a Data Strategy, and which stakeholders need to participate in this process?

At the heart of everything is business value. If there is no business value, then everything else collapses. So, the number one person to include in the strategy project is the ultimate end user. In many cases, the data strategist has a hard time making the connection between the Data Strategy and the enhancement of business value. This is a good indication that there is a problem. In every case, there needs to be a strong connection between Data Strategy and the enhancement of business value.

How would you recommend a new Data Governance lead create awareness and get buy-in from Senior Management on the relevance of building an integral and horizontal Data Strategy as the foundation for a successful Data Management program?

The most motivating factor in the corporation is pain. There are lots of pains. There is the pain of past failures. But most of all, there is the pain of failure in the marketplace – of finding new customers, of keeping existing customers, of growing revenue, and so forth. So, the best strategy for getting a project off the ground is to find pain and address the ways that the pain can be alleviated.

2. Data Management Maturity Model: Key to Data Strategies

Maturity ... is letting things happen.

Carolyn Heilbrun

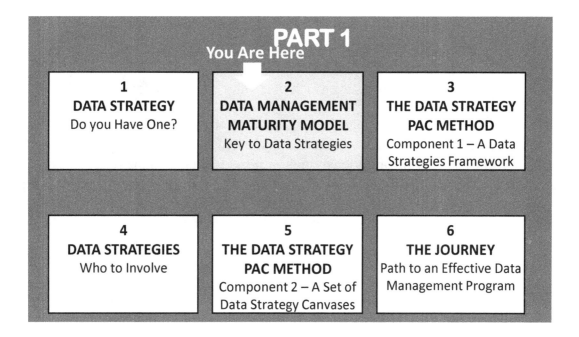

2.1.   Benefits of a Data Management Maturity Model

Before explaining why Data Management Maturity Models are important to Data Strategy, we must first understand what a Maturity Model is. Maturity models have been around since the mid-1970s to measure the ability and effectiveness of people to perform processes for specific disciplines. They were first defined to solve software development problems that increased with the growth of the use of computers. The first staged maturity model was developed by Richard L. Nolan, who in 1973 published the Stages of Growth Model. Watts Humphrey began the definition of his process maturity model concepts in 1986 and published in 1988.[24] From the Business Process Management perspective, maturity models are based on the assumption of predictable patterns of organizational evolution through the evolution of capabilities in a stage-by-stage manner following a logical path.[25] The concept of stages through which a specific discipline evolves and the idea that each stage includes specific qualitative and quantitative characteristics has been applied to Data Management. Several models have been developed to describe what it means for an organization to improve its Data Management capabilities and how to measure its progress in building these capabilities.

Data Management Maturity Models not only help us to assess where an organization is at a particular moment in any of its Data Management disciplines (e.g., Data Governance, Data Quality, Data Architecture, etc.), but they also can and must be used as a guide to define the roadmaps that will take us to the desired state on the way we treat data in an organization. These models can be used to:

- Assess the current state and diagnose an organization's level of maturity
- Identify existing gaps toward the desired state
- Define the progression toward maturity
- Clarify expectations for each stage (including what is left for later)

There are two ways to assess Data Management maturity: by asking people how they perceive the current state and by collecting evidence of maturity. The first is usually done by having stakeholders from different organizational units respond to a questionnaire. The caveat is that the results will depend on the respondent's exposure to the discipline assessed (e.g., Data Governance, Data Quality, Metadata Management, etc.). The second method involves collecting information (e.g., documents, processes, artifacts, emails, minutes, etc.) that shows what Data Management processes are being executed and to what degree. This evidence itself must be interpreted.

We obtain many benefits from the consistent and standing use of a Data Management Maturity Model. When defining Data Strategies a Data Management Maturity Model contributes to:

- **Common Understanding**: In Chapter 1, we asserted that Data Strategy helps manage expectations on Data Management. This includes establishing consensus on the definitions of mature Data Management practices. A Maturity Model contributes to this understanding, as it clearly defines what type of evidence should be in place for each maturity stage.

---

[24] History of Capability Maturity Model https://bit.ly/3uHZ6xg. The Software Engineering Institute developed the five-level Capability Maturity Model for Software in 1987. It evolved into the CMM IntegrationTM (CMMI), still focused on software development. Several models applied to different disciplines came after that.

[25] Maturity Models in Business Process Management https://bit.ly/3O2XuF6

- **Standardized Practices**: When following a Data Management Maturity Model, inventing required capabilities is unnecessary. The capabilities have been defined and standardized based on the experience and best practices of practitioners from diverse sectors. While there is room for customization of the artifacts, templates, and tools used to support the capabilities, the model itself will define most of what is required.

- **Anchor Guide for Roadmaps**: If Data Strategies are the highest-level definition of prioritizing data-related actions, a guide to the required capabilities is still needed. The capabilities indicated at each maturity level anchor organization-specific milestones in roadmaps and operating plans.

- **Managing Expectations**: Conflicts can arise in any relationship when expectations are not communicated or not fulfilled. A typical scenario in Data Management is not clearly understanding what Data Management means. A Data Management Maturity Model clearly indicates expectations at each level of maturity for each function represented in the model. Therefore, the Maturity Model can help articulate and manage expectations by indicating what to accomplish at each stage of Data Management implementation.

- **Alignment of Teams**: Clearly expressing what capabilities will be established in each phase not only helps manage the expectations, it also enables these activities to be aligned and coordinated across the diverse teams involved in the process.

- **Support During Audits**: External audits are a constant in highly regulated sectors (e.g., financial, insurance, health, etc.). Data Governance is becoming a common thread in audits. Recognizing weaknesses identified in a Data Management Maturity assessment and indicating in a roadmap when those will be solved will generally give positive points in an audit.

2.2. Maturity Model Options

Several maturity models have been developed that apply to aspects of Data Management (see Table 2). The model I'm most familiar with is DCAM. I've deeply studied it as I helped to translate version 2.2 to Spanish. DCAM was first defined in 2014 by members of the Enterprise Data Management Council. The EDM Council, created in 2005, is a not-for-profit organization aimed at elevating the practice of data and analytics management and supporting the role of the data professional.[26] It operates through membership of enterprises. It facilitates industry collaboration on Data Management and analytics research, best practices, standards, training,

---

[26] EDM Council https://edmcouncil.org/

and education. While it started with primarily financial organizations, today it includes over 300 members, representing a wide array of industries and regulators worldwide.

Most of the authors of the first version belonged to the Financial Sector. Their goal was to collect best practices in Data Management to comply with the recommendations of the BCBS 239, the principles for effective risk data aggregation and risk reporting, issued by the Basel Committee on Banking Supervision after the 2008 financial crisis.[27] Through recent years DCAM has evolved, and today many public and regulatory organizations and enterprises from very different sectors use DCAM.

DCAM can guide Data Management implementation in an organization. It describes the capabilities and actions required to acquire, produce, handle, and maintain trustworthy data. It includes the measurement and evaluation of strengths and weaknesses. Most importantly, it defines implementation roadmaps based on milestones for establishing the capabilities required as a backbone of Data Strategies.

Table 2 Alternatives of Data Management Maturity Models

Name	Abbreviation	Author	First publication	Most recent release
Gartner Enterprise Information Management Maturity Model[28]	EIMM	Gartner Group	2008	2016
Data Management Maturity Model[29]	DMM	CMMI Institute	2014	Retired by ISACA on January 1st 2022, to be subsumed in the CMMI Model
Capability Maturity Model for Research Data Management [30]	CMMRDM	Syracuse University	2014	

---

[27] BCBS 239 https://bit.ly/3csR5Gt

[28] Gartner Introduces the EIM Maturity Model https://bit.ly/3zbo4aS

[29] Data Management Maturity Model Introduction https://bit.ly/3coOX2t

[30] A Capability Maturity Model for Research Data Management https://surface.syr.edu/istpub/184/

Name	Abbreviation	Author	First publication	Most recent release
Data Management Capability Assessment Model[31]	DCAM	Enterprise Data Management Council	2014	Version 2.2 released on October 2021
Modelo Alarcos de Mejora de Datos (Alarcos Data Improvement Model)[32]	MAMD	Alarcos Research Group and La Mancha Castilla University, Spain	2018	Version 3.0 published May 2020

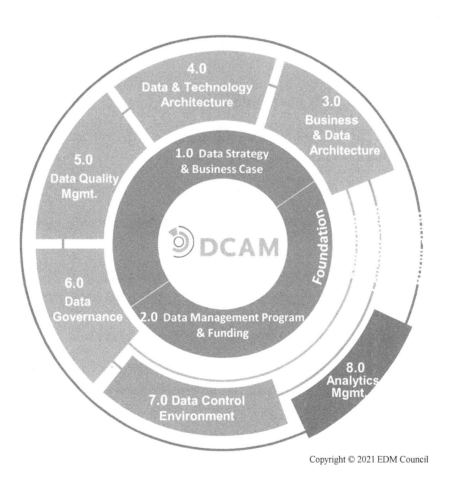

Copyright © 2021 EDM Council

Figure 8 DCAM 2.2 Framework

---

[31] EDM Council DCAM https://bit.ly/3PDW5Gw

[32] Alarcos Group MAMD 3.0 https://bit.ly/3aOucN2

DCAM 2.2 (Figure 8) comprises seven main components and an optional component (Analytics Management). Each component contains capabilities and sub-capabilities. Each has clear objectives and proposed artifacts to consider as evidence of an established capability or sub-capability. The eight components include 38 capabilities, 136 sub-capabilities, and 488 objectives.

Most maturity models, despite the processes they measure, use a maturity scale initially defined by the CMMI and included in the DMM (refer to section 2.2):

1. Performed
2. Managed
3. Defined
4. Measured
5. Optimized

DCAM does not follow this five-level format. It includes six maturity levels (Figure 9):

1. **Not initiated**: The capability/sub-capability is not established, and there is no awareness of its need. Only ad-hoc efforts might be found.

2. **Conceptual**: The capability/sub-capability does not exist, but there is awareness of its need; this is being discussed in various forums.

3. **Developmental**: The capability/sub-capability is being developed.

4. **Defined**: The capability/sub-capability has been defined and validated by directly involved stakeholders.

5. **Achieved**: The capability/sub-capability is established and understood across the organization and followed by the stakeholders. At this level, evidence of different types of artifacts (process documentation, policies, standards, emails, meeting minutes, etc.) can be found to sustain the achievement of this maturity level.

6. **Enhanced**: The capability/sub-capability is established as part of the business-as-usual practice and goes through a continuous improvement process.

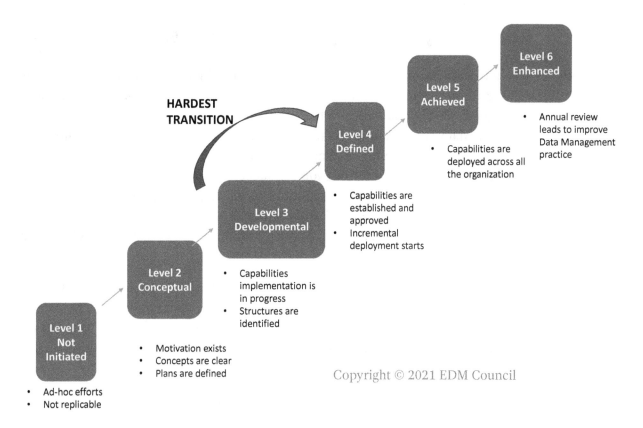

Figure 9 DCAM Maturity Levels

What I like most about DCAM is its Component 1 Data Strategy & Business Case. For DCAM, Data Strategy is fundamental to successfully implementing Data Management. DCAM recognizes that without a Data Strategy, there would not be a clear order on how to implement Data Management. According to DCAM 2.2, "the Data Management Strategy & Business Case determines how Data Management (DM) is defined, organized, funded, governed and embedded into the organization's operations." Data Management is expensive, and it is not a project. It is a series of functions that must be established and maintained. That requires annual funding. This is the relevance of having a Data Strategy and the definition of a Business Case upfront as a core foundation for Data Management.

Given that defining a Data Strategy is the first step to implementing a Data Management practice, the capabilities of a Data Management Maturity Model need to be accounted for in the Data Management Strategy. While any Data Management Maturity Model can be used for **The Data Strategy PAC Method**, I will refer to DCAM because it is comprehensive, well thought out, and mature.

2.3.   Relevance of Capability-Based Maturity Models

In Chapter 1, we said **Data Strategies** are the highest-level guidance in an organization for intelligently assigning resources to work in an integrated way to achieve data-related goals and business strategic objectives. The main idea behind this definition is prioritization. The list of things to do around the data ecosystem is so large that we need a means to identify the most important things to focus on. We have said that Data Management can be the foundation for other initiatives' success. Overall, it is a foundation for successful advanced analytics. Thus, we first need to prioritize the Data Management capabilities to develop and implement. To do this, we first must be very clear about what a good and mature Data Management practice means. Here is where a reference to a Data Management Maturity Model based on capabilities becomes most relevant.

Capability is "the quality or state of being capable" (Merrian Webster Dictionary, 2022); it implies, very simply, "the ability to do something" (Britannica Dictionary, 2022). When capabilities and associated artifacts are well defined (e.g., any document, minutes, distribution lists, etc.), it becomes easier to assess the level of maturity based on evidence rather than subjective perception.

Some of the benefits we can find in a Data Maturity Model based on capabilities are:

- Standardized capabilities are defined based on industry best practices.

- Capabilities allow comparison with other organizations in the same industry.

- Capability definitions allow a shared understanding of the maturity level of Data Management within an organization. It is evident and tangible what to do to move from one level of maturity to the next one.

- It is easier to define the backbone of a roadmap, with core milestones for capabilities establishment. Then we can set business-specific milestones around these core milestones.

- We can objectively measure progress based on the evidence described in the model.

- For our purpose, and as will be shown in Chapter 5, using a Data Management Maturity Model based on capabilities will help us prioritize which capabilities will be established in the short, mid, and long term, enabling management of expectations.

2.4. Key Concepts

Data Management Maturity Models are important tools for measuring the evolution of the different disciplines of Data Management.

Data Management Maturity Models based on capabilities are recommended to objectively measure maturity based on evidence.

2.5. Things to Keep in Mind

1. Data Management Maturity Models can be used as a guide to define the roadmaps that will take the organization to the desired state for the way we treat data.

2. A Data Management Maturity Model based on capabilities can help to set and manage expectations for good and mature Data Management practices across the organization.

3. Capabilities considered in a Data Management Maturity Model will work as a guide for prioritization in Data Strategies and as the backbone for the roadmaps derived from Data Strategies.

2.6. Interview on Data Strategy

EXPERT INTERVIEWED: **Melanie Mecca**[33]

Melanie Mecca is the world's leading authority on evaluating Enterprise Data Management capabilities.

CEO of DataWise Inc., she was recognized as a 'Leading Data Consultant' by CDO Magazine in 2022. She has unparalleled expertise and experience leading Data Management Assessments, benchmarking Data Management programs, and strategic roadmaps. Her leadership in evaluating, designing, and implementing Data Management programs has empowered clients in all industries to accelerate their success.

DataWise is a proud partner of the Enterprise Data Management Council and is accredited in the Data Management Capability Model (DCAM). As ISACA/CMMI Institute's Director of Data Management, Melanie was the managing author of the Data Management Maturity (DMM) Model

---

[33] Melanie Mecca https://www.linkedin.com/in/melanie-a-mecca-1b9b1b14/

and has led 38 Assessments to date, resulting in rapid capability implementation. DataWise provides in-depth instructor-led courses, utilizing case studies and numerous team exercises.

DataWise also offers a suite of eLearning courses for organizations, imparting key concepts and hands-on practical skills for broad staff audiences, elevating the organization's knowledge, establishing a data culture, fostering increased collaboration, and empowering governance. Stakeholder education is the key to Data Management excellence! Visit *datawise-inc.com* to find out "What **GOOD** Looks Like."

Given your vast experience as a consultant and practitioner in the creation of Data Management Programs and as the managing author of the Data Management Maturity (DMM) Model, what do you think is the relation between a capability-based Data Management Maturity Model and a well-defined horizontal Data Strategy guiding the data-related work and responding to business strategy? Have you found this type of Data Strategy in the organizations you have worked with?

Organizations setting out to establish, or enhance, their Data Management program are advised to conduct a comprehensive Data Management Assessment across the enterprise. The assessment provides a precise benchmark for current capabilities enabling the organization to discover strengths and gaps and develop a customized implementation plan to accelerate their progress.

I've found that organizations use the term 'Data Strategy' inconsistently, but typically, they emphasize technology transformation. In my experience, there are three primary components of an organization-wide Data Strategy:

- Data Architecture – WHAT needs to be designed and implemented to satisfy data requirements – (data models, data component plans, transition plans, etc.)

- Data Technology/Platform – the HOW – what the organization builds or buys to capture, store, and distribute data (emphasis on enterprise data / shared data)

- Data Management – WHAT processes need to be operationalized to build, sustain, and control the data, and WHO performs them – people, roles, and collaboration structures (governance).

From the Data Management perspective, I advise clients to develop the Data Management Strategy as a separate dedicated effort. Otherwise, it will almost always get short shrift, and be subsumed by 'shiny objects' (technology) and to some degree, by the target data architecture.

Basically, data is <u>forever</u>, you need to manage it effectively <u>forever</u>, and that implies establishing a permanent function, like Finance and Human Resources, supported by executive leadership, policies, processes, standards, staffing, and governance. Both the DMM and the DCAM emphasize development of a horizontal, broad-based, and sustainable Data Management program, based on a comprehensive Data Management Strategy. Because many organizations have not yet committed to this significant transformation, data-centric efforts and implementations may remain project-based, inefficient, and costly due to rework and redundancy.

What topics should be addressed in the Data Management Strategy? At a minimum, it should include:

- A <u>vision</u> statement (described above – aka, 'data Nirvana' for the organization), with an overall summary and the business aspirations for data assets that achieving the vision would enable

- Core <u>operating principles</u>, such as 'minimize redundant data,' 'data first design,' 'rationalize before build,' etc.

- Program <u>goals</u>, aligned with the organization's business goals

- Defined <u>objectives</u> to achieve EDM Program goals

- <u>Data asset scope</u> – (addressed above) – high-level <u>data domains</u> which are the focus of the Data Management Program

- Major <u>gaps</u> – summary of the current state of data assets and management practices, and the negative impact they cause in achieving business goals and objectives

- <u>Data Management scope</u> – the Data Management business processes that are required to attain business goals and remediate gaps (e.g., business glossary, data profiling, data catalog, etc.)[34]

- <u>Key work products</u> that need to be produced, such as policies, standards, and defined processes

- <u>Business benefits</u> – these should be described:
  - Satisfy use cases – e.g., predictive analysis of potential Product sales based on season, geographic area, economic factors, demographic trends, etc.
  - Improvements – e.g., to customer service, regulatory compliance, product development, etc.

---

[34] See the Data Management Maturity Model's list of 25 process areas and the Knowledge Areas in the Data Management Body of Knowledge to ensure completeness – note that the DMM focuses on fundamental EDM practices. At the same time, the DMBOK also includes solution areas (e.g., content management).

> - Tangible benefits – e.g., minimize maintenance costs, reduce quality defects causing delays in closing the books, ROI for faster development, etc.

- <u>Priorities</u> - how priorities, both for data domains and Data Management processes, are determined and what factors are involved – e.g., dependencies, business value, alignment to strategic initiatives, and level of effort

- <u>Governance structure</u> – a high-level description of governance roles, governance bodies, and how they interact

- <u>Business engagement</u> – how data representatives will be deployed to define data, build, enhance, and control the data assets

- <u>Staff resources</u> – estimate of resources required, and new positions to be filled – for example, the Data Management Organization, a Chief Data Officer, etc.

- <u>Metrics</u> – how will you know you're achieving program objectives? An initial high-level set of progress and component process metrics should be set out in the strategy

- <u>Benchmarking</u> – what method and Data Management reference model the organization will adopt to achieve an objective measure of capability development and implementation

- And last, but definitely not least – a <u>high-level sequence plan</u>, several years in duration, showing the major initiatives to be implemented.

The takeaway is, no matter what architecture you're aiming at or what technology you'll be purchasing to support it, you will always have to manage the data effectively. Once the Data Management Strategy is socialized and approved, it can be combined with Architecture and Technology for an overall Data Strategy.

What do you think is the role of Data Strategy in the success or failure of a Data Driven Transformation initiative?

'Data First' – that should be the guiding principle for every organization, whether a 100+ year old company seeking to further its business goals by leveraging its data assets, or a new startup aspiring to conquer its industry. Nothing happens without data – no business processes can be performed; no business decisions can be made.

"Failing to plan is planning to fail." Organizations would be wise to take the time to plan their Data Driven future. If they take the path of implementing several different capabilities without an overall strategy, efforts are subject to redundancy and less likely to be coordinated (not to mention more expensive). The strategy is the <u>antidote</u> to haphazard efforts.

I advise clients not to take too much time creating their Data Management strategy. The essential achievement which determines success (yes or no) is to obtain consensus and agreements from the major business lines or organizational units. The details can be fleshed out in the overall sequence plan for transformation, and the specifics required for capability building are then described in the implementation plans.

One element of the Data Strategy must be determined early top-down and emphasized – data governance. The strategy development effort is the occasion for structuring and implementing governance, without which the Data Management program cannot succeed.

From your perspective, who do you think should drive the creation and maintenance of a Data Strategy, and which stakeholders need to participate in this process?

If the organization has already funded and stood up a centralized Data Management Organization (DMO), it should be led by the top data executive of that organization – the CDO or equivalent. The key approvers should be the executives of the business lines/mission areas and information technology. They should designate senior representatives to work on the effort, and other enterprise-focused organizations should also be included, such as Analytics, Risk, Enterprise Architecture, Internal Audit, etc.

The DMO is the backbone, advocate, and maintainer of <u>persistent data products</u>, including:

- Data Strategy (Management, Architecture, and Technology)

- *Data Quality Strategy*

- Metadata Strategy

- Business Glossary

- Enterprise (or Business Area) Logical Data Models

- Data Management Policies, Processes, and Standards.

The CDO should work with peer executives to designate data working groups with members knowledgeable in the different disciplines, for example, to develop the data architecture, key players would be at least one enterprise data architect, business and technical data stewards, and a number of experienced data architects drawn from major repositories and critical operational systems.

How would you recommend a new Data Governance lead create awareness and get buy-in from Senior Management on the relevance of building an integral and horizontal Data Strategy as the foundation for a successful Data Management program?

This is the key question, isn't it? How to nail the internal sale of an enterprise-wide effort.

First, I would recommend that you study the organization's business strategy (or five-year plan, for Federal and State agencies). For each of the primary business goals, analyze the corresponding future state of the data assets that is necessary to meet those goals.

For instance, one goal of a software product company might be to increase customer retention by 25% in the next three years. Some of the data implications of that could be timely and accurate customer master data, analytics to identify factors associated with retention (e.g., product sales by customer correlated with retention), improved customer support call categorization and tracking, and expansion of self-service features on the customer-facing web portal. All of these examples are dependent on advancing the current state of the data.

Then, I would advise interviewing all of the business line / mission area executives and the CIO to discover:

- What they could do if they had the right data, at the right time, and in the right condition – that is, their <u>aspirations</u> with respect to data. If possible, get them to estimate the value if these aspirations were realized.

- What their major data <u>problems</u> are – either current or anticipated. And explore what the current inhibitors or obstacles the current state of the data causes, quantifying as much as possible.

The results of these interviews reveal the polarity between where they are, and where they want to be – goals to attain, problems to solve. Your analysis, in the light of the overall organization's strategy, will point you to the future state and what the Data Management, technology, and architecture need to deliver.

Finally, you present your findings and recommendations, and demonstrate how an integrated Data Strategy will advance the organization and how it will resolve persistent issues. This approach will ensure that every key voice is heard, synthesized, and reflected in your rationale for the Data Strategy.

3. The Data Strategy PAC Method: Component 1 - Data Strategies Framework

---

Strategy is about making choices, trade-offs; it's about deliberately choosing to be different.

Michael Porter

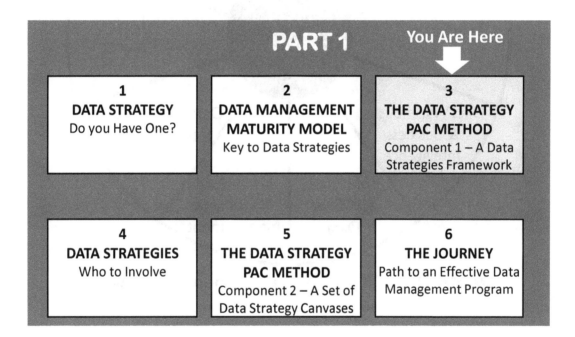

3.1. Frameworks: Sources of Inspiration

According to the Merriam-Webster Dictionary, a "framework is a basic conceptional structure (as of ideas)." The Thesaurus defines a framework as "the arrangement of parts that gives something its basic form." A definition I like more is from Cambridge Dictionary: "A framework is a supporting structure around which something can be built."

The purpose of a framework in a particular subject area is to provide a reference, a starting point. Instead of reinventing the wheel, we must use the existing wheels and dedicate our efforts to creating additional value. When the subject is Data Management, there is no better wheel than DAMA's Wheel (Figure 10), the Data Management framework where Data Governance sits in the middle, interacting with all the surrounding Data Management knowledge areas (or, as I prefer to call them, functions).

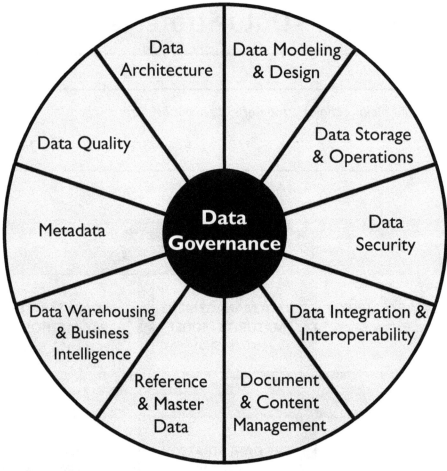

DAMA-DMBOK2 Data Management Framework

Copyright © 2017 by DAMA International

Figure 10 DAMA Data Management Wheel

The DMBoK2 includes an evolved version of the Wheel (Figure 11). Data Governance is no longer at the center of the Wheel. Instead, it encircles all the Data Management knowledge areas. In this version of the Wheel, we can see how all the Data Management slices we had in the original Wheel are arranged according to the stage of the data life cycle where they are more relevant. We also can see that Data Governance is no longer focused on defining policies and standards but on promoting all the concepts of the circle. The strategy is the most relevant from my perspective, as all the rest can be derived if well addressed in the Data Strategy.

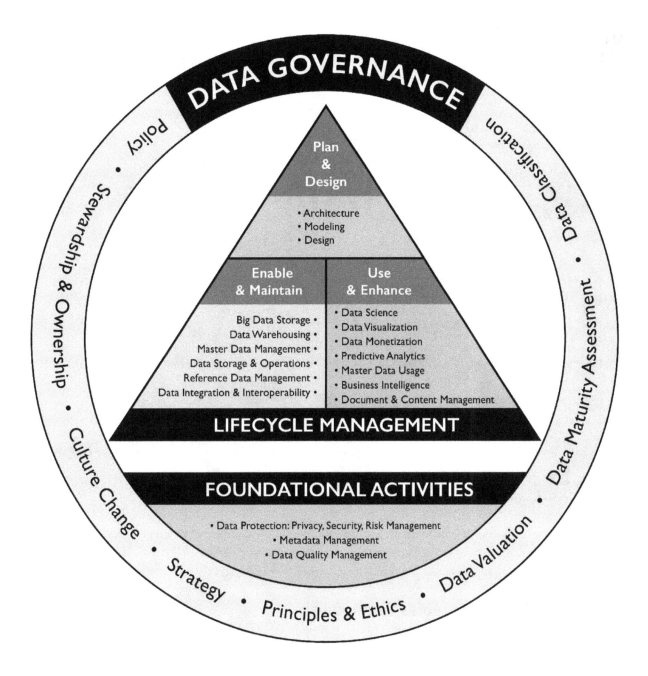

Figure 11 Evolved DAMA Data Management Wheel

Based on the representation of Data Management in Figure 11, the Data Governance lead is the orchestrator, but not the author, of the Data Strategies, as will be discussed in Chapter 4.

As described in Chapter 1, one of my sources of inspiration was Global Data Strategy, Ltd.´s (GDS) Framework, inspired by Donna Burbank (Figure 12). As this framework makes clear, the driver for Data Strategy is alignment with business strategy. The arrangement of the Data

Management functions in the middle of the diagram and the acknowledgment of different types of data at the bottom all point to the idea that the purpose of Data Strategy is to guide the priority of Data Management disciplines applied to specific data sources based on Business needs.

Figure 12 Global Data Strategy, Ltd.´s (GDS) Framework, inspired by Donna Burbank

3.2.   Data Strategies Framework

In defining a *framework,* we describe the structure for building Data Strategies. Yes, "strategies" is plural because we need a set of strategies. First, we need a strategy to define the data required to solve business needs. This way we ensure data aligns with business strategic objectives. In addition, the level of Data Management maturity drives the prioritization of how to implement Data Management overall. As an overarching function, Data Governance must also have a defined strategy. Then, because of their complexity, each Data Management discipline needs its own strategy. The different levels of Data Strategy include:

- **Data Alignment Strategy** where data domains are aligned with Business Strategy Objectives.

- **Data Management Strategy** where Data Management functions are prioritized.

- **Data Governance Strategy** where Data Governance capabilities, structure, and objects to govern are prioritized.

- **Specific Data Management Function Strategy** where each Data Management discipline gets its capabilities, structured, and data domains prioritized.

These all must be closely related to IT strategy, where all the technology platforms appear.

The Data Strategies Framework (Figure 13) illustrates these relationships. This framework shows all the elements to consider in a Data Ecosystem at a strategic level:

- The four types of Data Strategies mentioned above (Data Alignment Strategy, Data Management Strategy, Data Governance Strategy, Specific Data Management Function Strategies).

- Other relevant strategies (IT Strategy, Change Management Strategy, Communication Strategy) should exist and tie to the Data Strategies.

- Different types of data sources (at the bottom)

- The two most critical components of the data landscape:
  o Transactions as the leading producers of structured data
  o Analytics as the primary data consumer

Every element of this framework must be related and aligned.

- Top-down alignment ensures everything is linked to and derived from the Business Strategy.

- The execution of the strategies happens bottom-up.

- Horizontally, the alignment must be bidirectional between each element.

Defining a Strategy is not an easy thing. Because it takes work, we need to complete it in a very pragmatic way. Your goal is to produce a strategy that people in the organization understand and use – not something that sits on a shelf or in a folder. Thus, the core of **The Data Strategy PAC Method** uses a specific canvas for each Data Strategy highlighted in Figure 13 (Data Alignment Strategy, Data Management Strategy, Data Governance Strategy, and Specific Data Management Function Strategy). We will explore them in detail in Chapter 5. For now, let us begin by stating the purpose and content of each different Data Strategy.

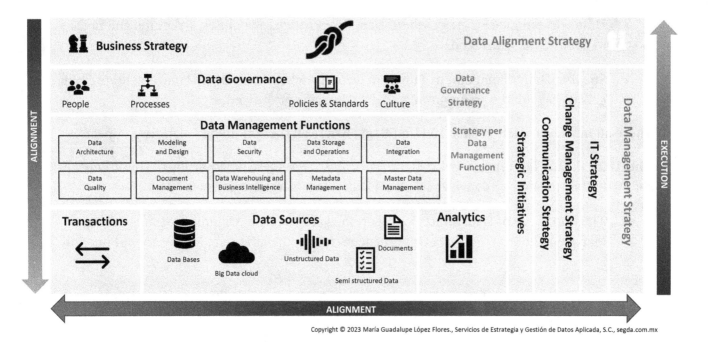

Figure 13 Data Strategies Framework

Each Data Strategy is defined to respond to the current state inputs: Motivations for better handling data, Data-Related Behaviors, and Data-related Pain Points (Figure 14):

- **Motivations:** These statements represent why the organization wants to establish or reinforce a Data Management program. Examples of these motivations could be:
  - To have accurate data to produce reliable insights and customer knowledge.
  - To have accurate data to improve customer experience.
  - To reduce the risk of not being compliant with local regulations.

- **Data-Related Behaviors to be Modified**: Becoming a Data Driven organization depends on creating Data Culture. An effective Data Management program involves processes, technology, and people. Oftentimes processes fail by not considering people. Data Strategies must address actions that people currently do and are not going in the expected direction when talking about handling data. Examples of these not-desirable behaviors are:
  - Producing reports without documenting data sources used
  - Not using authorized data sources
  - Not documenting metadata

- **Data Pain Points**: One relevant input the Data Strategies must respond to is represented by the current data-related issues. Some examples are:
  - Increasing fines due to poor-quality data delivered to the credit bureau
  - Duplicated customers are impacting cross-selling effectiveness
  - Reports produced by Sales are inconsistent with those produced by Finance

All these inputs must be prioritized, based on the level of their potential impacts (operational, financial, legal), to guide the prioritization of the actions to be described in the Data Strategies.

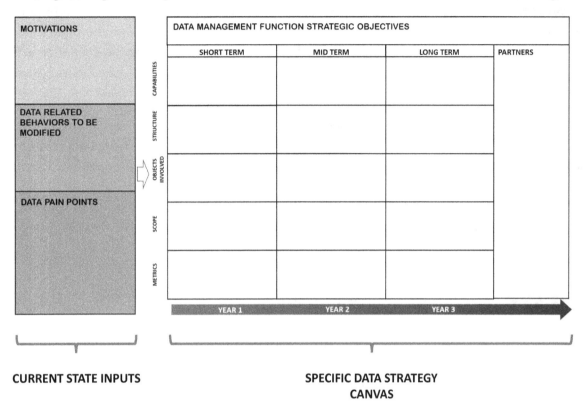

Figure 14 Inputs to Data Strategies

3.3.   Data Alignment Strategy

Start by aligning with the Business Strategic Objectives (e.g., 15% increase in customers, 10% increase in profitability, 5% increase in Net Promoter Score, etc.). This sounds obvious, but we need to understand what that means. The Data Alignment Strategy identifies the data the organization needs to execute its business strategy.

If there are gaps between what the organization needs and what it has, then one goal of this strategy is to address them. For purposes of the strategy itself, it does not matter whether the data exists within the organization. If there are gaps, that is a problem the strategy must plan to solve. There is a bidirectional alignment here. In Figure 13, from left to right, the Business Strategy must set the direction the organization has to take. It represents the fundamental input for the Data Alignment Strategy. From right to left, identifying requirements for new data or business insights from current data could help identify new business opportunities.

This first Data Strategy also identifies the producers and consumers of the data required. The data domains (e.g., customers, products, providers, employees, invoices, etc.) identified must respond to the Business Strategic Objectives, the business motivations, and, more importantly, the business data pain points. Here is where the challenges start. Although the inputs indicated in Figure 14 typically exist, they are often not documented. Sometimes the challenge is harder when the Business Strategy is not documented. Stakeholders must agree on the three top strategic statements that guide their work.

As we will explore in Chapter 4, to produce this first Data Strategy, we need the participation of stakeholders representing all the different organizational units. They all have data requirements and data pain points. This Data Alignment Strategy sets the foundation, for example, for the data principles and the value proposition behind managing data that stakeholders must agree on. Coming to a consensus is no easy task, but we can complete this with agility. In Chapter 5, we will discuss the specific canvas for each Data Strategy included in this Framework.

3.4.   Data Management Strategy

Once the Data Alignment Strategy is defined, the next thing to do is prioritize what to do from the Data Management perspective. This includes consolidating the data pain points identified and prioritized by the stakeholders participating in the strategy definition. Add the organization's motivations for having a Data Management program or a Data Driven transformation initiative. As a third input, list people's data-related behaviors that need to be changed. We will see in Chapter 4 that the stakeholder group that defines the Data Management Strategy will be smaller than the one that defines the Data Alignment Strategy.

One important topic to prioritize is the Data Management functions that will be formally addressed – those in the middle of the framework (Figure 13). Each box represents one of the DAMA Wheel slices. When I teach Data Management based on the DAMA Wheel, people frequently tell me they do not know where to start working. They get overwhelmed once they understand what each slice of the Wheel implies. Here is where the Three Leg Stool or the tripod theory based on Euclidian Geometry has a relevant role in the story.

The theory says that a well-produced 3-leg stool will be more stable than one with four legs. This is also the principle of tripods. The reason is straightforward, but to explain it, we must resort to the axioms of Euclidean geometry. We know that a plane is a two-dimensional surface formed by an infinite number of points of coordinates "X" and "Y" located at the same dimension or "Z." According to Euclid, three points are sufficient to define a plane because of the union of those points with lines. This means that the minimum expression of a plane or surface is a triangle. When a stool has four legs, different planes or triangles form with the combination of three points, so if the surface is somehow irregular, the stool will wobble.

Using this analogy, no more than three Data Management functions can be addressed formally at the same time if we want to succeed and make some good progress. Those are the stool's three legs, and one is always Data Governance. The other two legs are defined based on the top priority data-related pain points. This is a practical hint to prioritizing what Data Management functions to work on. This is captured in the Data Management Strategy, generally defined with a three-year horizon. So, each year, we can change one or two legs of the stool. This, of course, is not a rigid rule but a pragmatic and realistic recommendation.

Some other aspects require prioritization. We have said that, following the theory of the three-leg stool, one of those three legs will be Data Governance. Well, the first thing to prioritize is the establishment of Data Governance capabilities. Chapter 2 discussed the benefits of following a Data Management Maturity model based on capabilities to guide this part of the Data Management Strategy. But we also need to prioritize which data domains to focus on in each stage (short, mid, and long term). We must prioritize the data sources that will be managed.

One benefit of prioritization is to manage expectations across the organization on what to achieve with the Data Management Program. So, it is also relevant to list the ongoing strategic initiatives to leverage to start applying the selected Data Management functions. We also need clear visibility of the Data Management initiatives and what we expect them to achieve. Furthermore, finally, we need to identify the metrics that will let us know if we are progressing as expected.

3.5. Data Governance Strategy

When we complete the overarching prioritization of the Data Management Strategy, it's time to jump into the Data Governance Strategy, the one leg of the stool that we always need to work with. None of the strategies in this framework is isolated. They are interconnected but focused on different topics. The Data Governance Strategy's core purpose is to make clear what to expect from the team working in this function. I have seen over the years that most conflicts arise due to poor communication and failure to manage expectations. So, the Data Governance Strategy aims to define the scope and precisely set short-, mid-, and long-term priorities. It must include what to do to make clear what will not be done. Except for the Data Alignment Strategy, which starts by identifying the top business strategic objectives, the rest of the Strategies identify the specific strategic objectives for the topic the strategy covers (Data Management, Data Governance, Data Architecture, Data Quality, etc.). These strategic objectives, the motivations to have a Data Management program, the behaviors to modify, and the data-related pain points are the inputs to the Data Governance Strategy.

The categories to prioritize include:

1. **Capabilities:** Based on the organization's Data Management maturity model (see Chapter 2), we must segment the prioritized Data Governance capabilities into three

phases (short-, mid-, and long-term). The capabilities recommended by the selected Data Management maturity model anchor the roadmap. Around these capabilities, we add ones specific to the organization, such as create the inventory of data-related policies, include data policies in the enterprise policies management process, and so on.

2. **Structure:** Structure refers to the different roles we expect to have in the short, mid, and long terms. This includes the different roles and the number of anticipated resources (Data Governance leader, Data Quality leader, Metadata Management leader, three customer data stewards, one data modeler, one architect, etc.). It also includes the governing bodies (Data Governance Council, Data Stewards Committee, Glossary working group, etc.).

3. **Objects to Govern:** Prioritization of objects to govern sets the scope of Data Governance. Here is where the meaning of governing data must be grounded in its purpose to support business objectives. These items could be data domains (customers, products, invoices, etc.); processes (sales, account opening, data acquisition, data provisioning, etc.); data sources (data warehouse, data lake, master data, etc.), or even reports (profitability, claims, etc.).

4. **Organizational Units in Scope:** Usually, the highest priority organizational units to engage with are those with the most significant data pain points and are, therefore, most likely to benefit from Data Governance work. Set expectations as to which areas will wait until the mid- or long-term. Implementing governance all at once (the big bang) is complicated and likely to fail.

5. **Metrics:** How we plan to measure the progress and effectiveness of the Data Governance work. Metrics must evolve, based not only on the scope and complexity of the indicators but also on the capabilities implemented. One example of this is the indicator of policies. Perhaps in the first year, we want to measure the progress and completeness of the written and approved policies against the list of expected ones. In contrast, the compliance indicator with the policies is more suitable to be found over the long term once we enforce the policies.

Identify the partners that will help us move forward in executing the Data Governance Strategy. An example of a great partner is a business unit lead, someone at the Senior level with the highest impact or pain points due to the lack of Data Governance. They will be among the earliest beneficiaries of this practice. Institutional Internal Communication is another example of an organizational unit we want to have as a close partner.

3.6.   Specific Data Management Functions Strategies

Once expectations for Data Management and Data Governance are defined strategically, a strategy should be defined for each Data Management function, starting with the other two legs of the stool. The strategy should be based on the motivations and pain points and connected to business objectives. The inputs for these Data Management Function Strategies are the same as in the Data Management and Data Governance Strategies: Motivations, Data-Related Behaviors to be Changed, and data-related Pain Points. The first step, again, will be to define the strategic objectives for the function.

The categories to prioritize include:

1. **Capabilities:** The capabilities will depend on each Data Management Function we are working with and the phase we are in. Let us say we are defining the Data Strategy for Data Quality. Some of the first capabilities to address could be establishing the Data Quality Management process, creating and approving a Data Quality Program, and generating a process to identify critical data elements. These capabilities are the ones likely to be suggested by your Data Governance Maturity Model. Some additional and specific capabilities would need to be identified and prioritized, like inventorying business-critical processes, enabling profiling, and root cause analysis.

2. **Structure:** This section lists the specific resources we expect for each phase related to the Data Management Function for which we define the Strategy. Continuing with the Data Quality example, perhaps in the short term, we only expect a Data Quality lead and a Data Quality analyst. Still, in the mid-term, we expect to have two data profilers, three Data Quality analysts, and five data stewards.

3. **Involved Objects:** Define the scope and set the expectations of what to address for the Data Management Function we are describing. In the same Data Quality example, we could prioritize the Critical Business Processes for which Critical Data Elements will be identified and monitored.

4. **Scope:** Set expectations for and be very clear on what is within the scope of each phase (short, mid, and long-term). To continue with our example of Data Quality, we may want to limit the scope of Data Quality to customer data.

5. **Metrics:** Metrics link the strategy with the way it is executed. Here we prioritize the indicators and measurements we will have over time, which may vary depending on the Data Management Function we are discussing.

3.7.   Role of IT Strategy

Because data production and use are technology-dependent, it is critical to understand Data Strategies in relation to IT Strategy. IT representatives will be among the stakeholders defining the Data Strategies (to be discussed in Chapter 4). Still, once the Data Management Strategy is defined, it needs to be discussed with the IT team to ensure IT Strategy supports Data Strategy goals. For instance, if the Data Management Strategy identifies the need to establish the Metadata Management practice in the short term, then we must ensure that the IT Strategy includes evaluating and implementing the Metadata Management infrastructure in the short term. Of course, we must also align IT Strategy with the Data Governance Strategy. This way, it should include evaluating, acquiring, and implementing the technology platforms required to support the Data Governance Strategy.

3.8.   Role of Change Management Strategy

Many Data Management practices are new to some organizations, at least in a governed and articulated way. This means they require that people change how they work. So, it is valuable to have the support of the Change Management unit within the organization if it exists. The Data Strategies must be socialized with the Change Management team and aligned with the corresponding strategy if it exists. Identifying and training the "change champions" are vital components linking the Data Strategies with the Change Management Strategy.

3.9.   Role of Communication Strategy

If you asked me to give a standard recommendation for all the Data Strategies we have discussed, it would be the 3C recommendation: communicate, communicate, and communicate. Strategies in general and Data Strategies in particular, must be democratized. Everyone in the organization should feel connected with the Data Strategies and have them easily accessible. If a corporate or institutional Internal Communication area exists, socialize the Data Strategies with them. Align with their strategy and leverage the existing infrastructure so our communication efforts do not collide with their communication campaigns.

3.10.   Strategic Initiatives

Most organizations have a strategic initiative in place. An initiative strong enough to move the whole organization. For example, digital transformation, transformation to a Data Driven organization, a merging, or even a divestiture. Håkan Edvinsson calls this "Gravity," meaning that "something is moving in the organization. Something is rocking the building with enough energy to get people's attention" (Edvinsson H. , 2020).

Since these initiatives are top priorities, they are usually good candidates to start delivering the value of the Data Governance discipline and the specific Data Management functions to prevent data-related pain points.

3.11.   Data Sources

Data sources are objects that are subject to governance. Different types of data sources exist, including transactional databases, operational databases, historical data repositories, and unstructured data sources. Within the unstructured data, we can find the audio recordings of a call center and customer opinions on the Internet and emails. Data sources must be prioritized to steer Data Governance actions.

Eventually, all different data sources need to be governed. Below is a suggested way of classifying data sources for prioritization for governance (note: These are not necessarily mutually exclusive):

- **Databases**: Usually are relational, but we can still find hierarchical ones related to legacy systems. These are mostly populated and updated by transactional systems.

- **Big Data Cloud**: Refers to data repositories primarily for operational support and analytics. These typically combine structured, unstructured, and semi-structured data. Usually, we will find these repositories stored in clouds but given that this classification has more to do with technology, we can also include here on-premise repositories.

- **Unstructured Data:** Refers to non-structured data sources in audio, video, or text. For instance, the audio recordings from a customer support call center. These can be textualized and then analyzed to be converted into meaningful structured data. Unstructured data can be divided into repetitive and nonrepetitive unstructured data (Inmon, Lindstedt, & Levins, 2019).

- **Semi-structured Data**: This does not conform to a data model but has some structure. It lacks a fixed or rigid schema. The data does not reside in a relational database but has some organizational properties that make it easier to analyze. With some processes, we can store them in the relational database (Geeks for Geeks, 2021). Examples are emails, XML files, TCP/IP packets, and binary executables.

- **Documents:** Data can also be found as physical documents, which can be digitalized, stored, and managed through a document management system.

3.12.   Transactions

We must consider two main components of the data ecosystem when defining Data Strategies: Data Producers and Data Consumers. The Transactional environment produces most of the structured data. This comprises business processes supported by transactional systems and people using these systems, running the day-by-day business. Transactional data is usually stored within normalized tables within Online Transaction Processing (OLTP) systems and designed for integrity. It is generally integrated into data repositories to be prepared for further consumption by the Analytics environment. Transactional data can also be provided by sources external to the organization. When defining which objects to govern, it is essential to have a high-level understanding of this environment to understand how different data sources are populated.

3.13.   Analytics

When asked why Analytics is not within the Data Management Functions area, I answer that it is not part of Data Management. This has been a philosophical discussion as they are both very tightly related. Since analytics professionals do so much work to find, understand, and clean data, some people may think this is another discipline of Data Management. I categorically say it is not. Data Management is all you must do along the data life cycle to ensure data is healthy and in good quality condition for consumption. Analytics is data consumption to get business insight, predict the future, and even prescript what to do. Analytics professionals are consumers of data; they are customers of Data Management.

I compare it to fine dining. The Chef aims to create great culinary experiences so that people who enjoy his food can tell inspiring stories. You have a great experience when you are offered a creative dish (architecture and design) with excellent quality ingredients (quality) combined in a unique and balanced way and with a great wine pairing (integration). You never expect to get ill with the meals you receive (security), and all the experience is completed with the service (operations) and the explanation of what you are getting (Metadata). But the cooking and plating (visualization) are what make the ingredients ready to be consumed (analytics), and its success strongly depends on all the previously mentioned elements (Data Management).

3.14.   Key Concepts

Data Strategies Framework is a structure to visualize the different types of Data Strategies to be built, indicating how they relate to each other and other existing strategies in the organization.

3.15.   Things to Keep in Mind

1. Data Strategy is not singular. It is plural. It is a set of different Data Strategies, each one with a different perspective.

2. All Data Strategies must be tightly related and aligned with other existing strategies in the organization (Business Strategy, IT Strategy, Change Management Strategy, and Communication Strategy).

3. The main goal of Data Strategies is to prioritize the use of limited resources over time and to set clear expectations. Data Strategies must be democratized so that they are easy to find, understand, and use throughout the organization.

3.16.   Interview on Data Strategy

EXPERT INTERVIEWED: **James Price**[35]

James Price is a Data Management thought leader with over 30 years of experience in the information industry. Internationally recognized as an author and presenter, he is the founder of Experience Matters, a firm that helps organizations protect, and maximize the value of, their data, information, and knowledge, to address the problem that, whilst Information Assets are vitally important to organizations, by and large, they are very poorly governed and managed. His work with the University of South Australia has been described by Gartner, the world's most influential IT industry advisory firm, as "tremendous" and the research as "ground-breaking." He's co-author of the Leader's Data Manifesto and Chair of the Leaders Data Organization (*www.dataleaders.org*).

You have vast experience as a consultant in the Data Management and Data-Related world. How often do you find a well-defined horizontal Data Strategy guiding the data-related work and responding to business strategy in your customers' organizations?

The Oxford Dictionary defines a strategy as "a plan of action designed to achieve a long-term or overall aim." For the avoidance of doubt, I use the broadest definition of data; it includes all data, documents, records, published content, and knowledge. A well-defined Data Strategy will aim to deliver the right (high-quality) information to the right people (not the wrong people) at the right time (in a timely and easy-to-access fashion).

---

[35] https://www.linkedin.com/in/james-price-experiencematters/

A well-defined Data Strategy will address the ten domains identified in the paper entitled "Information Asset Management in organizations: Development of a holistic model" which can be found here:

https://www.experiencematters.com.au/wp-content/uploads/2021/07/Information-Asset-Maturity-Model-2021.pdf

Our global research shows that addressing each of these domains is critical to the success of the strategy.

Very rarely do I find a well-defined horizontal Data Strategy guiding the data-related work and responding to business strategy in your customers' organizations. Many organizations have a Data Strategy that addresses the domain of the Information Asset Environment, which includes data governance and the domain of Information Systems. Very few organizations have a Data Strategy that addresses the remaining eight domains.

What do you think is the role of Data Strategy in the success or failure of a Data Driven Transformation initiative?

A Data Strategy is a critical guide to a Data Driven Transformation initiative. It provides the roadmap of how to reach the initiative's goals.

Digital transformation is about customer centricity and frictionless business. You can't do either without efficient and effective Data Management. How can you have customer centricity if you don't know who your customers are? How can you have frictionless business without instant access to the data, information, and knowledge you need to make business decisions and to process transactions?

A Data Strategy should articulate the organization's current business and data practices, the business implications of those practices, the organization's vision of the future and how to get from where the organization is to where it wants to be. A Data Strategy is a critical enabler to a Data Driven Transformation.

From your perspective, who do you think should drive the creation and maintenance of a Data Strategy, and which stakeholders need to participate in this process?

To determine which stakeholders need to participate in the process of creating and maintaining a Data Strategy, it is vital to understand the difference between business governance, asset governance, and asset management. Governance is about oversight and control. Business governance is about who makes what decisions. Asset governance is about making those decisions and implementing them. Asset management is about the day-to-day operations.

When governing the organization, the Board and Chief Executive Officer (CEO) make the decision of who is going to be made accountable for the management of its financial assets and they appoint that person to the position of Chief Financial Officer (CFO). The CFO is made truly accountable for the financial assets and, if the CFO mismanages the organization's money they will be sacked, and if (s)he misappropriates it they will be jailed. There is true accountability.

When governing the organization's financial assets, the CFO develops the financial strategy and annual budget, carefully delegates financial authority, and measures and reports on income and expenditure.

When managing the organization's financial assets, the people with delegated financial authority are responsible for spending the organization's money in line with the financial strategy and annual budget.

The model is identical for data, information, and knowledge assets. The Board and CEO should make somebody accountable for the quality of the organization's data. That person, the data equivalent of the Chief Financial Officer, perhaps the Chief Data Governance Officer, needs to govern the data. It is this person who should be accountable for the Data Strategy and the instruments and delegation required to manage data well. And the responsibility for managing data assets well rests with every person in the organization. Regarding roles, we should not get hung up on the difference between data owners, data custodians, data stewards, and so on; it just muddies the waters. Clear accountability and responsibility are what is required.

How would you recommend a new Data Governance lead create awareness and get buy-in from Senior Management on the relevance of building an integral and horizontal Data Strategy as the foundation for a successful Data Management program?

Awareness and buy-in from senior management are mandatory. We have just discussed the difference between business and asset governance and management and who does what – the governance should be done by the organization's most senior management.

But there is more to it than that. There is no point in investing on a project basis; for transformation to be successful, it needs continuous improvement in the management of data, information, and knowledge. Continuous improvement needs continuous investment. Continuous investment needs continuous measurement of data quality and the ensuing business benefits. When justifying investment, no Chief Financial Officer will even look at a business case unless they perceive a business problem. Once the problem has been identified, the CFO must be convinced that an acceptable return on investment will be achieved. And the CFO will only reinvest if the projected benefits are realized, not only for the initial project, but over time.

4. Data Strategies: Who to Involve

The diplomacy approach strives to reduce the formalities and omit the coercive parts of traditional Data Governance.

Håkan Edvinsson

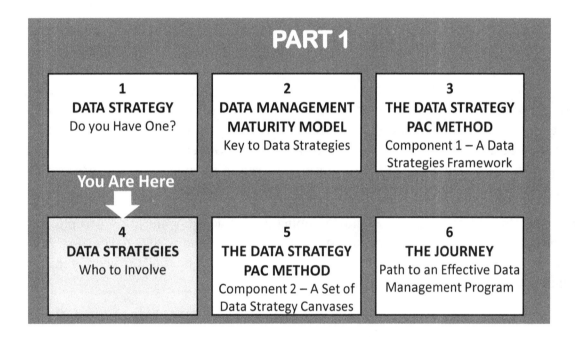

4.1.   Who Should Define Data Strategies?

Generally, business strategies are defined exclusively by a limited number of top management people. The elite. Business strategies are rarely widely communicated across the organization due to a veil of secrecy. "Data Strategy" if something with that name exists, is often focused on technology as defined by top IT management. It would more accurately be called "technology strategy." But we want an integrated Data Strategy fully aligned to business strategy, considering all parts of the organization, addressing data needed, principles, value proposition, capabilities required, prioritization of resources, strategic initiatives, and metrics, with all responding to business needs and data-related pain points. So, who should define it?

During my early years in IT at a Bank, I witnessed how, every year, a very select team went on a Tech Tour to explore new technologies to support Business Strategy, which was, on the business side, defined by another select team. The results could have been broadly communicated but they were not. And this is the story of many organizations. If we look back in history, the core idea behind strategy was to keep it secret. As Sun Tzu advised in the 5th century BC, "Conceal your dispositions, and your condition will remain secret, which leads to victory; show your dispositions and your condition will become patent, which leads to defeat.

We often think of strategy in terms of competition with other organizations. That is part of it – getting a competitive advantage means you do not show your hand. But it is also vital that the organization can EXECUTE the strategy. That means the people in the organization need to understand it. Unlike Sun Tzu's approach, I think Data Strategies have to be democratized, not concealed. They should be clearly defined, widely communicated, and accessible to everyone who uses them. Democratizing Data Strategy requires engaging data creators/producers and data consumers in a collaboration that serves the organization's best interest. The Data Strategies Framework (Figure 13 in Chapter 3) shows that representatives from across all the business units and shared services must define the Data Alignment Strategy (the highest data strategy level). These representatives must be able to speak for their data-related pain points. As illustrated in Figure 15, the type and number of direct stakeholders decreased as we defined the detail of the other Data Strategies (Data Management Strategy, Data Governance Strategy, and each Data Management Function Strategy). But since the Data Alignment Strategy drives the other strategies, the connection to the horizontal requirements remains.

The book, *Open Strategy,* describes how winning companies stay ahead of disruption through openness (Stadler, Hautz, Matzler, & Friedrich von den Eichen, 2021). The first case study describes Ashok Vaswani's approach to strategy when, in 2012, he took the helm of the UK retail business Barclays:

Vaswani believed there was a better way to define strategies. If rank-and-file employees had a hand in crafting strategy from the beginning, they'd feel more invested in it, understand it better, and do their best to execute it. Meanwhile, leaders would be able to craft more nuanced plans if they had exposure to front-line concerns, and they'd be able to communicate the strategy better.

This was exactly how I approached Data Strategies! Data Strategies must be open and represent the organization holistically. Achieving openness starts with identifying who should participate in defining each Data Strategy. As described in Chapter 7, the recommended approach to define Data Strategies is through workshop sessions.

Figure 15 illustrates how to identify stakeholders to contribute to Data Strategy definitions. Details will differ across organizations. Although this model was developed for a mid to large organization, small to medium organizations can also use the model. As you identify stakeholders, account for who addresses different aspects involved in running the organization, such as operations, finance, governance, marketing, and so on. Approach this process with the sense of openness required to define each type of Data Strategy, as described below.

Data Alignment Strategy: As discussed in Chapter 3, it should be defined first because it drives the other strategies. This process will identify:

- The data domains required to address the organization's motivations (business strategic objectives)

- Data-related behaviors to be modified or adapted

- Data-related pain points.

This requires representatives from across the organization (different lines of business [LOBs], Finance, Legal, Human Resources, IT, Data Governance, any data-related unit, Enterprise Architecture, or similar unit with an overarching view of the organization, etc.). Data pain points can exist everywhere.

Stakeholders defining the Data Alignment Strategy must establish a common understanding of the 3-5 top-priority business strategic objectives. With agreement on strategic business goals, stakeholders can prioritize the motivation, behaviors, and data pain points. These priorities will be the primary input for defining the Data Management Strategy.

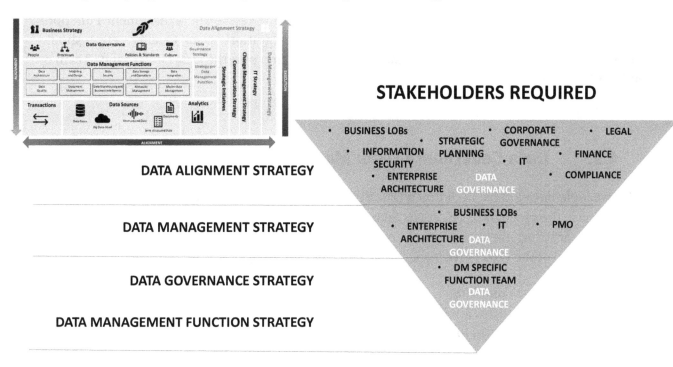

Figure 15 Data Strategies - Stakeholders Required

Data Management Strategy: The primary input to define the Data Management Strategy is the prioritized list of motivations for managing data, the data-related behaviors to be modified or adopted, and the data-pain points. We can identify business stakeholders for prioritizing the Data

Management functions based on the prioritization defined through Data Alignment. Complementing this team with the Data Governance team and IT stakeholders is mandatory. The Data Governance team will oversee the execution of the Data Strategies, and the IT team will need to support the technology required for effective and efficient Data Management. Enterprise Architecture will need to maintain an enterprise view that describes the holistic scope of the Data Strategy.

Data Governance Strategy: The Data Alignment Strategy and the Data Management Strategy provide input for the Data Governance Strategy, including prioritized lists of motivations, behaviors, and data-pain points. One goal of the Data Governance Strategy is to define the data and the objects to govern (e.g., regulatory reports, data repositories, business processes, etc.), as well as the capabilities that will be governed over time. This definition includes the roles required to execute capabilities.

Since Data Governance team members orchestrate the definition of Data Strategies, they will know and understand the Data Alignment Strategy and can use this to define the Data Governance Strategy. In keeping with the open strategy approach, all Data Governance team members contribute to this strategy, not just the Data Governance Lead.

Data Management Function Strategy: The stakeholders for each Data Management Functions Strategy (Data Architecture, Data Modeling, Data Integration, Data Quality, etc.) should comprise the team executing the Data Management Function plus the Data Governance Team or at least its leader.

4.2.   Data Governance Lead: Master Orchestrator

Many people have a stake in defining Data Strategies, but the process will not happen magically just because they recognize this stake. Someone must orchestrate the process of articulating the strategies, ensuring their execution, and evolving them over time. This orchestration is the responsibility of the Data Governance Lead. This role includes:

- Engaging stakeholders
- Ensuring strategies are documented
- Acting as custodian of the Data Strategies
- Socializing and communicating them
- Ensuring they get embedded in the Business's Annual Strategic Planning

These activities are required to treat data as a "strategic asset."

For years, the role of the Data Governance Lead has been tightly associated with producing policies and standards, overseeing the data ecosystem, and addressing data issues. In many organizations, the Data Governance team is perceived as coercive, imposing requirements that most people don't understand and see no purpose to. This creates considerable resistance to Data Governance initiatives and to following direction from the team. Håkan Edvinsson advocates for the benefit of bringing diplomatic principles to Data Governance. As he points out, "Focusing on data errors is to give data governance a very low ambition; it would imply moving from bad to no bad." (Edvinsson H. , 2020) The role of Data Governance should be much broader. It should guide the evolution of the data landscape and culture by facilitating the alignment of Business and Data Strategies.

If we look again at DAMA's Evolved Wheel (see Figure 11 in Chapter 3), the outer circle contains all the topics Data Governance must promote in the organization. This goes far beyond policies. In Figure 16, note that the outer circle includes the topic of Strategy, which reinforces my point of having the Data Governance Leads (and their teams) "orchestrating" Data Strategies.

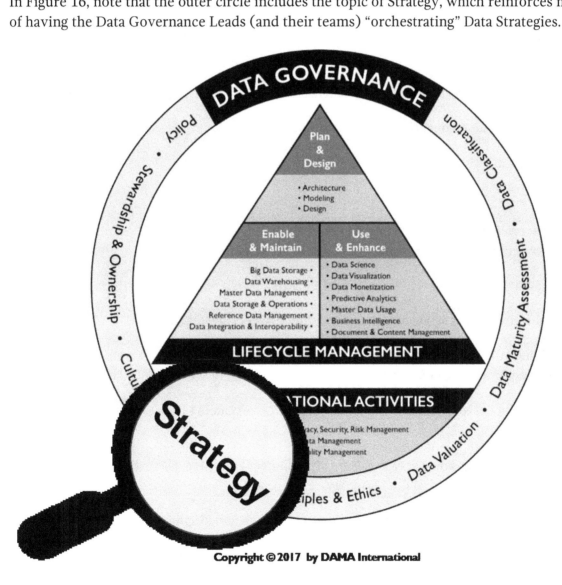

Figure 16 Strategy as one of the core Data Governance activities

The role of the Data Governance Lead in orchestrating the definition, communication, maintenance, and execution of Data Strategies is challenging. So is implementing an effective and sustainable Data Management Program. The biggest challenges include:

- Establishing leadership and commitment from top management

- Defining a clear Data Strategy and disseminating it widely

- Describing a business case for continued funding of the program

- Identifying critical data for which it makes sense to control Data Quality

- Planning for better data and getting people to implement plans

- Managing Metadata with the same attention as managing Data

- Developing a solid Business and IT alliance for Multi-Functional Data Management

- Managing Data throughout its Life Cycle

- Having the technology that allows effective and agile support

- Having an effective Communication Strategy

The Data Governance team significantly contributes to defining a clear Data Strategy (the second bullet). To overcome this point, some specific challenges appear:

- Engaging the right stakeholders to participate in the definition of Data Strategy

- Generating a Data Strategy aligned with the Business Strategy

- Guiding and monitoring the use of data in alignment with Business Strategy as part of the execution of Data Strategy

- Governing based on the principles defined when producing Data Strategy, to treat data as an asset

- Defining policies and a way to ensure compliance with them, according to the prioritization defined in Data Strategy

- Avoiding the creation of coercive governance while developing a sense of ownership

- Being flexible and achieving the appropriate degree of formality without falling into rigid controls that may be rejected

- Adopting a simple governance model that people can use while accounting for organizational culture and leveraging existing structures and processes

- Generating metrics that show the effectiveness of the approach instead of simply counting what is easy to count

- Assuring Data Strategy gets embedded into Business Strategic Planning

- Assuring Data Strategy execution

- Communicating Data Strategy, execution progress, and value effectively

Chapter 7 details the steps needed to produce the Data Strategies, communicate them, and embed them into Business Strategic Planning. The "Data Strategies Orchestrator" will be fundamental to the success of this process.

4.3.   Casting Stakeholders

As was discussed in section 4.1, it is essential to identify who must participate in defining the Data Alignment Strategy, as some of these stakeholders will also contribute to subsequent Data Strategies, such as Data Management, Data Governance, and specific function strategies. At this point, there's no strict requirement as to any stakeholder's level in the organization. Most importantly, each participant has some clout, possesses deep business processes knowledge, and understands data-pain points. Most likely, the team will include people from both leadership and operations. The core requirement is that people involved in this work fully understand the processes they are interested in and the data they need to support such operations. Overall, they must understand the problems they usually face regarding data. We can identify these key players by presenting the business case for producing Data Strategies at an existing Senior Management governing body meeting. It is essential to get leadership buy-in and commitment to get funding and to set priorities for stakeholders to participate in this process.

We'll see in Chapter 6 that before attempting to define a Data Strategy, we must ensure a basic understanding of data concepts across the organization and assess where the organization stands regarding Data Management practice. Today, most organizations have at least some Data Management functions. During training and maturity assessment sessions, we can invite some key players to define Data Strategies. Their participation in the training and assessment sessions reflects their knowledge and command of business processes and problems they usually face in data. So do not skip these training and assessment steps. These processes will also contribute to developing a common language around data, which is foundational for a data-based culture. Importantly, these current state sessions can help you identify people who can contribute to the strategies.

4.4.   True Sponsor is not Just a Funds Provider

Of course, to start working on Data Strategies, we need to have buy-in from Senior Management, which can be challenging. Most senior managers will say that data is critical and that it is a priority to have data to support business decisions. However, assigning key people to sit in meetings and define Data Strategies is another story.

But how can we get buy-in from Senior Management to work on a holistic Data Strategy? The clue is in the data-related pain points. As Håkan Edvinsson points out, not only are the current data-pain points significant but so are pain points that may appear along the road if a good Data Strategy is not in place. A strategic perspective helps an organization anticipate and mitigate the types of problems that are likely to arise from its choices. Therefore, we must focus on preventing long-term pain and addressing current pain. Like many people, when referring to physical pain, organizations want to solve a specific issue (e.g., users getting high response-time when accessing business intelligence reports or dashboards). They don't always think of preventing future problems. Most people I've contacted agree that having a good Data Strategy is important, but they don't create one because they think it takes too long and does not solve their immediate problems.

Many companies make significant investments in technological platforms to solve data issues, get accurate insights about the organization, and make better decisions. Much of the time, disappointment and frustration follow these investments. Almost all organizations have at least one story about the failure of an investment in technology to return value. These can be leveraged to document business cases for alternative approaches. This business case for developing Data Strategies should address the cost of the current data issues, the potential cost of not doing Data Strategies, and the value of a defined approach.

In the same way that a person could face severe effects if they continue to take painkillers without finding and properly treating the root cause of their pain, an organization can waste its time and talent if it fails to approach data strategically. We must find a way to describe the long-term consequences of this lack of strategic vision about data. Most organizations need an approach that combines immediate short-term relief and long-term prevention.

Finding the lead sponsor is essential. There's no rule about where the lead sponsor should be located, although it is always better if sponsorship is on the Business side rather than in IT. While funding is significant, it is not all we are looking for. We also need someone genuinely interested in seeing progress made, who can ask deep questions about the work done and share accomplishments and benefits with the organization in different forums. Other sponsors who do not necessarily provide funding can be strategic partners. These are generally senior managers from the business units where most data issues are found. They will participate in and support Data Governance or Data Management initiatives that reduce their pain. Once they feel the benefit, they will be the best advocates of the benefits of an exemplary Data Strategy in the success of any data-related initiative.

4.5.   Key Success Factors

While applying **The Data Strategies PAC Method** in different organizations, I've found some common success factors, including:

- **Get Buy-in on Data Strategy:** If top management is not convinced about investing funds and critical people's time in producing Data Strategies, it won't be easy to develop them, at least not in a holistic, horizontal, and open way.

- **Plan to Succeed:** Once there is buy-in, detailed and careful planning is required to honor the promise and do the work in a pragmatic and agile way. Extreme care must be given to scheduling meetings, sending invites properly, and ensuring invitees are well-informed about purpose, process, and time commitments. They should receive a powerful message from top management encouraging them to attend. Planning must include how to socialize outcomes, collect approvals, and broadcast the Data Strategies across the organization.

- **Get a Message from Stakeholder Recorded:** A three-minute video, including a strong message highlighting the relevance of data and how it is treated across the organization, will be a good, reusable asset for communications. This is a pragmatic and feasible way to open meetings with new audiences, with a strong message of commitment and encouragement to have better data in the organization. This will be of significant help in getting a commitment from stakeholders.

- **Run a Kick-Off Meeting:** An easy and pragmatic way to get stakeholders assigned to work on the Data Strategies definition is by doing a kick-off presentation at a standing management meeting. This time can be used to have the managers identify/commit stakeholders to do the work.

- **Level Set Data Management Concepts:** This is another vital aspect for facilitating stakeholders' participation. Begin with basic Data Management concepts level-setting. This will enhance the ability of stakeholders to define the Data Strategies and shorten the time needed.

- **Adopt a Data Management Maturity Model:** Whichever model is selected, using recommended Data Management capabilities as anchor milestones will help prioritize establishing and deploying disciplines along the timeline.

- **Engage Non-funding Sponsors:** During the definition of Data Alignment Strategy, it is very feasible to identify those non-funding but supportive sponsors. They need to be engaged first-hand to become advocates of Data Strategies.

- **Engage Institutional Communication:** If there is an Institutional Communication unit within the organization, they must be engaged at the earliest time possible in the Data Strategies initiative to help communicate the Data Strategies across the organization.

- **Create Awareness of Data Strategy Annual Cycle:** We must treat Data Strategies like other organizational strategies. We must revisit and adjust them every year. Stakeholders must understand their roles and responsibilities in this process.

- **Engage Strategic Planning:** To close the cycle, whoever oversees Business Strategic Planning needs to be engaged to ensure Data Strategies will be included in ongoing/annual planning.

 ## 4.6.   Key Concepts

Data Strategies Orchestrator is the person who identifies and engages stakeholders to participate in the Data Strategies definition. This role also includes facilitating the process, communicating the resulting Data Strategies, and overviewing their execution. This is usually the Data Governance Lead.

 ## 4.7.   Things to Keep in Mind

1. Key stakeholders must provide input and feedback when Data Strategies are defined.

2. The Data Governance Lead, or equivalent role, is best suited to orchestrate and oversee the participation of key stakeholders in defining Data Strategies.

3. Training and Data Management maturity assessment sessions are good forums to identify some key stakeholders to participate in the definition of Data Strategies.

 ## 4.8.   Interview on Data Strategy

EXPERT INTERVIEWED: Håkan Edvinsson[36]

---

[36] Håkan Edvinsson. https://www.linkedin.com/in/hakanedvinsson/

Håkan Edvinsson is a Data Management consultant specializing in Data Governance and Decision Modeling. He's the author of *Data Diplomacy*, where he suggests how business innovation and business transformation relate to non-coercive Data Governance. His key message is that this can be done by using a diplomatic approach, avoiding bureaucracy, and having the leanest Data Governance organization set up as possible. He's also a recognized trainer and speaker.

Given your rich experience as a consultant in the world of Data Governance and Data Architecture, how often do you find a well-defined horizontal (considering all the organization) Data Strategy guiding the data-related work and responding to business strategy in your customers' organizations?

It used to be rare, or even non-existent. Nowadays, large organizations quite often express their ambitions of having data as their vital "natural resource" from which fortunes are to be excavated. And lots of money and effort are put into it. One of my clients in the automotive industry has expressed that 50% of the income will come from services in 2030 instead of just from vehicles. Other clients are forming similar strategies. Not all industries are that progressive, though.

So far, the investments I come across are for Data Architecture and do not consider Data Governance. To be blunt, it's IT-centric, so I would not refer to it as "a well-defined horizontal Data Strategy" as such strategy, or its implementation, is too narrow.

As professor James H. Davenport put it: "At a plumbers conference no-one talks clean water" when referring to IT professionals as plumbers (focused on storages, pipes, and fittings).

What do you think is the role of Data Strategy in the success or failure of a Data Driven Transformation initiative?

I think that not separating the Data Strategy from other strategies in the organization is vital. The "data" is not a separate thing as the data reflects what is going on in an enterprise and what the organization deals with. A successful data-centric transformation requires profound insights in the data, which in turn is to have insights in the detailed business operations. My recipe is to not only involve business knowledge but to make the business responsible for it. It is a business strategy, not an IT strategy. This is applicable in any business transformation.

Ultimately, we do not need a Data Strategy; rather, we have business strategies that also consider data.

Just look at a utility company. It may purchase energy that they put into their grid and distribute to clients. Their entire business is actually data about the energy; how much did we buy and how much did our clients use? Measures from thousands of meters are gathered, processed, and then form the base for financial transactions. In such an environment, you never separate the energy from the data about the energy, in any step.

Organizations that are becoming data-centric now tend to miss this point simply because they never had this kind of data.

From your perspective, who do you think should drive the creation and maintenance of a Data Strategy, and which stakeholders need to participate in this process?

Let us start with what a strategy is; it is the expressed means for achieving desired outcomes in a long-term perspective. A strategy is always something that concerns the board level and thus decided on that level. I think that those who are active in data quality and data governance must give their input to the strategy, complementing the business IT oriented intentions. Roles like data governance leads, chief enterprise architects, and enterprise data architects should therefore influence a Data Strategy.

The most important aspect of a strategy is the implementation of it. A Data Strategy needs to be translated into project guidelines, job descriptions, performance indicators, and so on. In my experience, it is not unusual that everything seems to be in place but still nothing is happening. I therefore propose that a strategy must not only have indicators showing whether we are achieving it or not, and whether it is the right strategy or not. We must also have indicators showing if we actually are implementing it, or not.

My general principle is to have these indicators formed and kept alive near their natural source, such as close to the transformation initiatives when they are identified, planned, formed, executed, and evaluated. This would include roles like sponsors and project portfolio managers.

How would you recommend a new Data Governance lead create awareness and get buy-in from Senior Management on the relevance of building an integral and horizontal Data Strategy as the foundation for a successful Data Management program?

Do your homework; if data quality is an issue, how bad is it? What are the business implications from that? If the normal way of improving the data architecture is not helping it, then why? What is the outset for the transformation that, so far, is lacking from supervision of business data?

Before approaching the senior management, understand where they stand on this. What is their idea about the transformation that lies ahead of them? What do they know about the topic? Start where they are and use what is already there. For instance, their concerns, their challenges and what motivates them. Talk their language. If you must educate them to understand what you are proposing, you are on the wrong track.

5. The Data Strategy PAC Method: Component 2 - A Set of Canvases

---

Effective communication helps to keep the team working on the right projects with the right attitude.

Alex Langer

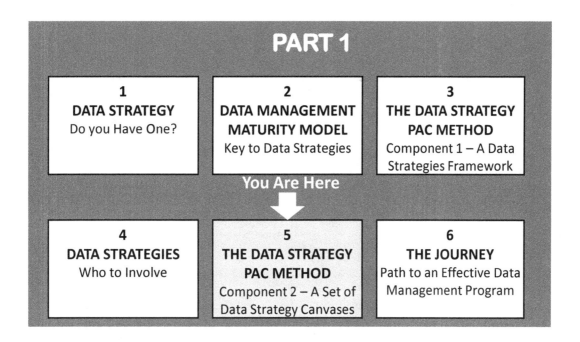

5.1. Business Model Canvas, the Core Inspiration Source

In Chapter 4, we discussed the importance of an open Data Strategy, one that many people contribute to, understand, and have a stake in, one that is democratized. Once we define Data Strategies, the next challenge is communicating effectively about them, especially to people who must execute them. While information fills our lives, we tend to read less. At least we dedicate less time to reading a single document. We keep going from one topic to another in a matter of minutes. Therefore, sharing relevant, synthesized information on a single slide is powerful. This need for synthesized information was addressed in *The Business Model Canvas*

(Alexander Osterwalder, 2005), which describes how to "paint" essential information about a business on a single slide (Figure 17).

I have been using the Business Model Canvas since 2006. First, for understanding what I must do when starting a new function in corporate life or when starting an entrepreneurial project. The technique helps me clearly understand who my customers are, what value proposition I can offer them, and through which resources and activities. From there, I can explain it to others straightforwardly.

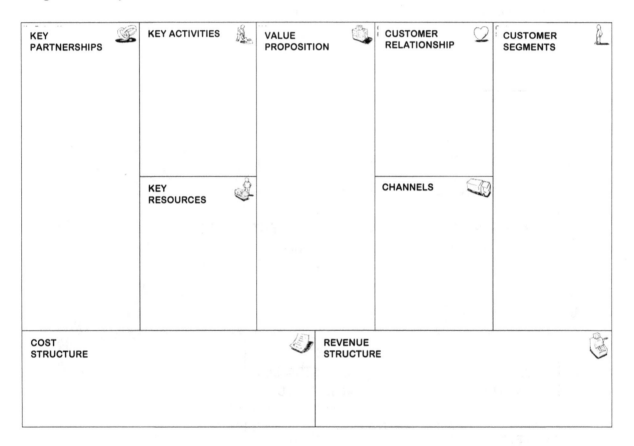

The Business Model Canvas CC License A. Osterwalder, Strategyzer.com www.strategyzer.com

Figure 17 Alexander Osterwalder's Business Model Canvas

The canvas concept has developed significantly since Osterwalder first described the Business Model Canvas. Strategyzer, the company Osterwalder founded, launched the Business Case Model Canvas.[37] Project Management professionals use Project Canvases.[38] Search the Internet, and you will find canvases for very diverse topics. All the Canvas Models share one common

[37] https://www.mbamanagementmodels.com/business-case-canvas/

[38] https://bit.ly/3dbW4Md

idea: simplify the communication of a model and increase the possibility of having a common understanding.

Some teams fail to coalesce and collaborate because they do not understand their core purpose: whom they serve and how they serve their customers. A canvas can help set expectations among the people involved in the activities described by the canvas and the customers of those activities.

This chapter will introduce and explain how **Data Strategy Canvases** can communicate different levels of the aligned Data Strategies described in Chapter 3. The goal is to describe each strategy in a single slide. Producing an effective canvas takes much back-office work. It requires synthesizing multiple inputs while keeping their meaning clear. (We will discuss implementation methodology in Chapter 7.)

5.2. Inputs to Data Strategies

Data Strategies must align with Business Strategies. Ensure that alignment starts with identifying the Business Strategic Objectives. These Objectives are not always documented. In a few cases, they may be published internally, but this is not generalized practice. More often, we need to ask about them because (as discussed in Chapter 4) they are wrapped in secrecy. Business Strategic Objectives are critical in the Data Alignment Strategy Canvas (see section 5.3). We must reference them when defining the Data Strategies described in Chapter 3 (The Data Strategies Framework).

While they are essential, Business Strategic Objectives are not the only driver of Data Strategies. Additional inputs include:

- Business Questions

- Data-related Pain Points

- Motivations

- Behaviors to be changed

These will not be found written anywhere and must be discovered through guided sessions with key stakeholders (see Chapter 4).

5.2.1 Business Questions

People at leadership levels throughout the organization ask questions daily. These are business questions related to their specific span of responsibility. In most cases, these questions can be answered with current information assets, such as reports, dashboards, and interactive applications. But answering them can take a long time (e.g., customer segmentation report being available two weeks after the end of the month). In other cases, the organization does not have the data required to answer the questions.

Some samples of such questions are:

- How does the current profitability of product x compare to its profitability two years ago?

- What's the profitability of branches in zones with the highest insecurity index?

- What's the average number of products bought by the same customer?

- What are the channels used by the most profitable customers?

- Is there a relationship between students' absences and their test scores?

- How many inactive customers have been reactivated in the last month?

- What infrastructure was used in the most profitable branches?

- What are the zip codes of the most frequent customers?

Listing and prioritizing questions from leaders across the business is the first step in identifying the type of data required to answer them, even if the data does not yet exist in the organization. When defining Data Strategies, we don't want to go to the data element level. Instead, start with broad categories of data (domains, such as customers, accounts, orders, providers, products, branches, etc.) needed to answer business questions. The priority of questions will influence the priority of data domains in the Data Management and Data Governance Strategies.

5.2.2 Data-related Pain Points

The data-related pain points are another important input to the Data Strategies. Start with issues that currently and directly impact the organization. For example,

- Inconsistent reports presented by Sales, Finance, and Operations

- An increase in fines incurred by a bank for submitting low-quality data to the Credit Bureau

- A low rate of customer contact ability by an insurance company

- Limited cross-selling capability

- Inaccurate inventory due to inconsistent methods of product identification

Each unit within the organization will have pain points. You will need to be very selective when addressing them. Those with the highest impact should be the top priority. Understanding impact and prioritizing action items require the participation of the same vital stakeholders that prioritized the Business Questions.

While you should start with current pain points, the process should also identify risks – problems that are not evident at this moment but can turn into severe pain points, with dramatic effects if they are not mitigated through the Data Strategy. For example,

- New or emerging compliance requirements

- Regulations that are not yet being addressed

- Initiatives to become global not considering other markets' regulations

- Lack of customer centricity

- Distributed management of product catalogs

5.2.3 Motivation

Two additional inputs will be required when defining the Data Management Strategy. The first one is Motivation. It is relevant to recognize and express what drives the organization to invest in Data Management. Whether the organization wants to become Data Driven or to recover market position through insight into customers' behavior, these motivations will help prioritize what aspects of Data Management the strategy must address.

5.2.4 Behaviors to be Changed

The last input needed for the Data Strategies is understanding how people in the organization behave around data. These behaviors describe how people interact with data, how they use data, and how they understand their responsibility around the data they are exposed to. Data Strategies need to address behavior to improve a data-oriented culture. Examples of this kind of input include:

- Reports designers do not document the data sources they use in their reports

- Data requirements are not correctly registered (i.e., business requirements are defined at the functionality level and do not include data)

- Project managers do not account for producing Metadata or managing data quality when creating the project's budget

- Solution designers do not refer to Enterprise Data Model (when it exists) to define/update data models at the project level

- Developers reuse existing fields in a data structure without documenting the change in purpose

As the examples show, these behaviors can be the direct cause of data quality problems.

5.3. Data Alignment Strategy Canvas

Figure 18 shows the canvas used to define the first Data Strategy, the Data Alignment Strategy. This is a critical strategy. Through it, we will align the business needs and strategic objectives with the rest of the Data Strategies.

On the left are the inputs to define the strategies. We always keep them in sight to ensure we remember what the strategies are responding to. Input to the Data Alignment Strategy includes prioritized enterprise strategic objectives, business questions, and data-related pain points.

Data Domains: The main objective of this first canvas is to identify the high-level categories of logically grouped data (Data Domains, such as customers, products, suppliers, and accounts) required to respond to business questions and to support the enterprise's strategic objectives, as well as those related to data pain points. All data domains identified must be listed, even if the organization does not have data for specific domains.

Data Providers: This is where we list the entities, understood as organizational units or external sources related to the identified data domains. We want to identify the high-level business processes where data is produced. Remember, this is the highest level of the Data Strategies, so we are not talking about what we know as data sources; those will come into the scene in other Data Strategies.

Data Consumers: Similarly, we need to identify those organizations (internal or external) or individuals that consume the data related to the domains listed.

Data Principles: Håkan Edvinsson describes the benefit of using principles, rather than rules, as the basis for Data Governance. Principles depend on trust and build trust because they connect to a common purpose. (Edvinsson H. , 2020) Examples of Edvinsson's principles include:

- Trusting people

- Always the right data from me

- Capture data close to the spot-of-origination

- Opportunity is power

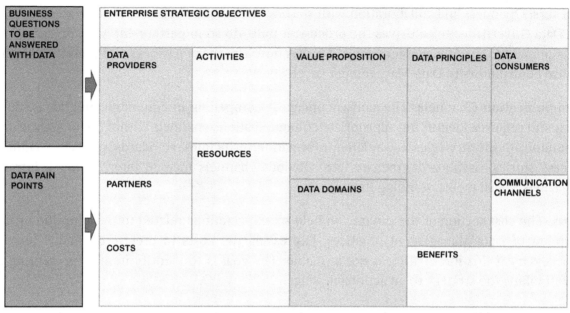

Figure 18 Data Alignment Strategy Canvas

This first Data Strategy must include the principles that guide behaviors around data. Everyone should follow them. For example:

- We respect the official source of each piece of data.

- We commit to ensuring the confidentiality, security, and integrity of other people's data, following standards we expect for our own data.

- Our data handling practices must consider respect for people, taking care to maximize benefits and minimize possible damages.

Value Proposition: Since this is the highest-level Data Strategy and the canvas will tell the story of what to do in the data arena, it is essential to define Data Strategy's Value Proposition. This value proposition supports the Data Strategies, in general, by asserting the value of better data handling across the organization.

Activities: Data Strategies set expectations for Data Management, resource requirements, and priorities. What to do to manage data, when, with which resources, and in which order. It is essential to be clear on the activities that drive a successful Data Management Program. This section lists high-level activities, including developing additional strategies in the Data Strategies Framework.

Resources: Data Strategies must link implementation to specific actions. This begins by identifying the people and material resources required to perform the activities required to make good on the value proposition. Data Management requires people. Getting resources later in the process is hard if we do not explicitly express the requirements as part of the strategy.

Partners: Openness and collaboration with stakeholders results in better Data Strategies. While the Data Governance team drives the process, it must do so in partnership with organizational units pursuing Data Management goals. This section lists those partners and identifies them as critical contributors to Data Management success.

Communication Channels: The canvas concept is compelling in communicating ideas. But to use it still requires identifying appropriate communications channels within the organization to communicate the strategies and related information: principles, standards, policies, roadmaps, success stories, dashboards, metrics, etc. Obvious channels include internal email, intranet, magazines, social media, standing forums, etc.

Costs: The cost section of the canvas can help set expectations related to the adoption or non-adoption of Data Management practices. Expressing the costs in precise economic terms is unnecessary if this information is not available. The goal is to identify items representing the cost of taking the strategy to an actionable stage.

Benefits: The counterparts of Costs are Benefits. The Benefits section should include both qualitative and quantitative benefits. As with Costs, if exact figures are unavailable, it is not mandatory to include them, but it is important to identify categories of benefit.

5.4.   Data Management Strategy Canvas

Once the Data Alignment Strategy is defined and documented, it is time to prioritize actions and resources to develop the Data Management Strategy canvas. At this moment, two additional inputs come into the scene: The motivations to establish a Data Management program and the data-related behaviors to be changed (Figure 19). The data-related pain points used as input to the Data Alignment Strategy are also crucial to the Data Management Strategy, so they appear again on the left of this canvas.

The Data Management Strategic Objectives, as defined and prioritized by stakeholders, head this canvas.

Columns (SHORT, MID, AND LONG-TERM): This canvas helps to allocate resources by including three columns: short-term, mid-term, and long-term. Typically, these columns can be represented by years, but this is not a rigid rule. Accounting for a logical progression of objectives over time is *"intelligently assigning resources to work in an integrated way to achieve data-related goals and contribute to achieving business strategic objectives."*

Partners: This section lists those organizational units and roles that are of core importance to the success of the Data Management program. This may include all or a subset of the partners listed in the Data Alignment Strategy Canvas, including Corporate Communication, PMO, Compliance, Enterprise Architecture, and so on.

Data Governance: All the Data Strategies need to be related. The link from this canvas to the Data Governance Strategy Canvas is the row labeled Data Governance. Here, we list Data Governance capabilities that we need to establish in the short- mid-and long-term. These capabilities are based on the organization's Data Governance Maturity Model. They may also include requirements specific to the organization. Data Governance appears in the first row of the elements to be prioritized because of its critical role in overseeing the other Data Management disciplines.

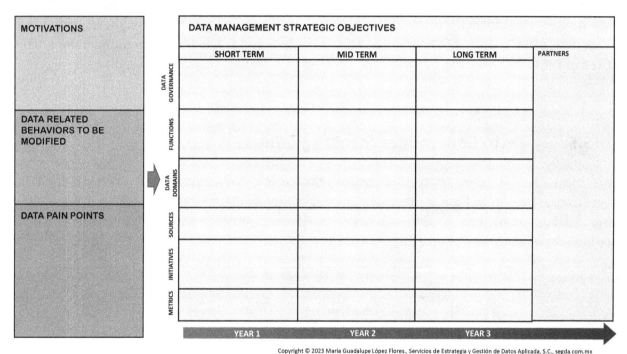

Figure 19 Data Management Strategy Canvas

Functions: This section refers to DAMA's Data Management Knowledge Areas: Data Governance, Data Architecture, Data Modeling and Design, Data Storage and Operations, Data Security, Data Integration and Interoperability, Data Document and Content Management, Master and Reference Data, Data Warehousing, Metadata, and Data Quality (Figure 10) (DAMA International, 2017). This canvas refers to them as Functions to transmit the sense of action and their goal to eventually become "business as usual."

Data Domains: We identified data domains in the Data Alignment Strategy Canvas. This section prioritizes over time short-, mid-, and long-term the application of Data Management Functions and Data Governance capabilities to these domains.

Data Sources: An essential part of prioritizing efforts and setting expectations is to indicate which data sources to address when Data Governance capabilities or Data Management functions are deployed. For example, the Data Domains row may show not only that Customers are a top priority but also that customer data to govern is the data in the Data Warehouse, the CRM, and the Master Database as authoritative sources of that data.

Initiatives: The best way to open paths for Data Management deployment is by leveraging ongoing strategic initiatives that have already been recognized as a high priority. These generally have approved budgets and the attention of key stakeholders. Listing them here associates the Data Management strategy with the business strategy. Getting the Data Management strategy approved will drive the engagement of people involved with these initiatives and drive the short- mid- and long-term adoption of Data Management practices.

Metrics: A strategy without action is worthless. To be understood, actions must be measured. The strategy must include clear KPIs to show it is implemented. This last row indicates how we measure the deployment of Data Governance capabilities and Data Management Functions. This row can show the evolution of metrics as the Data Management capabilities evolve.

5.5.   Data Governance Strategy Canvas

It is time to detail how we approach Data Governance. We can see it as a drill down into the Data Governance row of the Data Management Strategy Canvas (Figure 19). This canvas describes the organizational structure to support Data Governance, what elements to govern, and where within the organization (Figure 20).

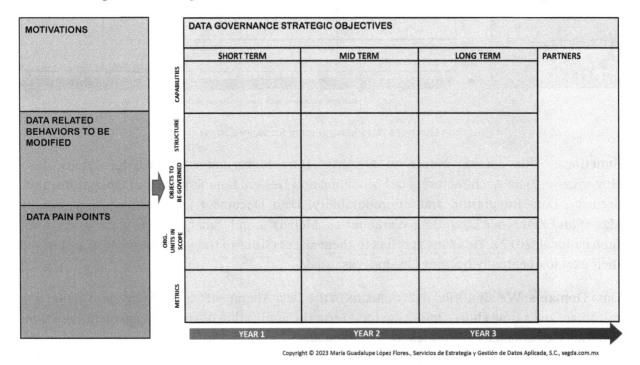

Figure 20 Data Governance Strategy Canvas

Precisely the same inputs we used for the Data Management Strategy Canvas we can transfer here to keep them present while documenting the content of this canvas. Like what happened with the Data Management Strategy, the Data Governance Strategic Objectives must be defined first by the stakeholders working on this Strategy.

Capabilities: This is the direct link to the Data Management Strategy. The same capabilities appear in the first row of both canvases.

Structure: Structure refers to the organization of the Data Governance function. Here, we must be clear on the roles and number of people required to run the program. At the start, we will likely find the Data Governance leader, two Data Governance assistants, and a few data stewards for selected organizational units in the short term. As the deployment of Data Governance expands to other areas, the number of data stewards and other staff may increase. The structure section is also the place to indicate the governance bodies. In the short term, we do not create a specific Data Governance body. Instead, we leverage standing governance bodies to promote the Data Governance program. For example, the Governance lead may request time on the leadership team's agenda to discuss data issues, report on the Data Governance initiative's progress, or request other input from senior management.

Objects to Govern: This section is critical to setting expectations for what the Data Governance team will do. Data Governance is still a very abstract concept for many people. At best, a general understanding recognizes that Data Governance defines data policies and then oversees adherence. Attempting to deploy Data Governance practices across the organization all at once usually ends in failure and can also increase resistance to the idea of Data Governance. Roll-out should be planned and intentional. It starts with identifying what objects to govern in the short-, mid-, and long-term. An object could be a business process, a data repository, a regulatory report, a data integration process, a data migration process, a data source, a data domain, etc. The short-, mid-and long-term columns will document different objects to govern. This communicates the concept of incremental deployment.

Organizational Units in Scope: Continuing with the idea of incremental deployment of the Data Governance practice, this row indicates the priority of the organizational areas that Data Governance will serve. Actions related to governing a unit may include identifying data stewards, training, enforcing policies, documenting business terms in the glossary, identifying critical data elements, documenting business Metadata, etc.

Partners: As mentioned for Data Management Strategy Canvas, we must list the organizational units or roles that will help adopt and deploy the Data Governance practice. Typical partners for Data Governance include the institutional Policies Unit, the Compliance unit, and Internal Audit, as they help facilitate the management and enforcement of Data Governance Policies throughout existing governance bodies and processes.

Metrics: This row will show the evolution and maturity of the metrics over time. In the short term, most KPIs relate to implementing and deploying the Data Governance processes, based on the organization's Data Management Maturity Model.

5.6.   Data Management Specific Function Strategy Canvas

Once the three Data Management Functions are selected according to the three-leg stool theory (Section 3.4), we must document each strategy (Figure 21). We maintain the same inputs (motivations, data-related behaviors to be modified, and data pain points) identified when documenting the Data Alignment Strategy. However, we should highlight those impacting the specific Data Management Function.

Capabilities: The organization's Data Management Maturity Model capabilities will appear in this canvas section and anchor the implementation roadmap. We can complement these with organization-specific capabilities. For example, if the Maturity Model does not include the specific Data Management Function (e.g., DCAM does not include Data Integration), the capabilities must be defined based on the processes and enablers required to perform them.

Structure: Each Data Management discipline requires the participation of different roles, some of which are common to other fields, like the data stewards, and will not need to be replicated here as we should include those in the Data Governance Strategy Canvas. In this row, include only the roles and governance bodies specific to the Data Management function described by the canvas.

Objects Involved: As was done in the Data Governance Strategy Canvas, identify objects on which the Data Management function will be applied. To illustrate, if the Function is Data Architecture and the Object is the Customers Data Domain, it means that Customers are the "thing" relevant to the organization we need to document as part of the Enterprise Data Model (EDM).

Scope: Defining Scope is critical to setting expectations. This row will show the short-, mid-, and long-term scope of the Data Management Function. For example, if, for Data Quality, the Objects Involved focus on the Customer Data Domain, we can limit the short-term scope to Customer contact data elements.

Partners: As described in previous canvases, this section lists the roles or organizational units identified as core partners in the execution of the specific Data Management Function.

Metrics: Metrics describe KPIs specific to the Data Management Function. If, included in the Data Management Maturity Model, the expected scoring for short-, mid-, and long-term should be included in the appropriate columns.

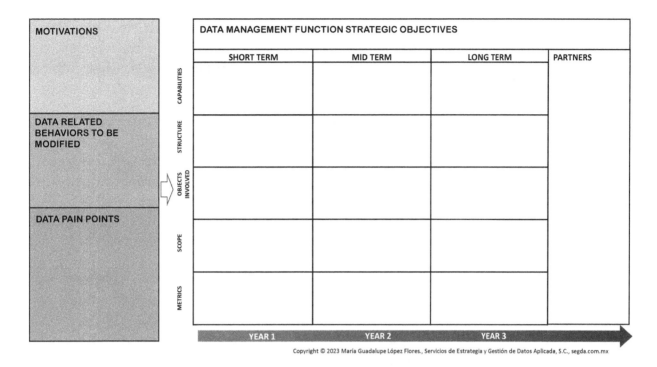

Figure 21 Data Management Function Strategy Canvas

5.7.   Data Governance Business Model Canvas

It is crucial that people in the organization, beginning with the governance team, develop a common understanding of what Data Governance means to the organization. The best way to communicate this is through a Business Model Canvas. See each Data Management Function as an individual business within the organization. It is fundamental for team members to know their (internal) customers, key activities, and their value proposition.

Note in Figure 22 that the Data Governance Business Model uses the same inputs as the Data Management and Data Governance Strategies Canvases.

Customer: The Data Governance team must clearly understand their customers, including organizational business units, IT development units, database administrators, the CDO, and so on. Customers must not be assumed. Explicitly identifying them helps focus on the work and how it must be oriented.

Value Proposition: After identifying customers, consider each group's value proposition. Value Proposition statements must resonate in the mind of the customers to move them to look for the Data Governance team's support and participation. Complement this section with the list of Data Governance services (What does Data Governance sell/offer to the customers?) through which we realize the value proposition. Making this connection helps make the abstract concept of Data Governance very concrete.

Channels: This section lists the means of communicating with customers so that they understand the Data Governance Business Model and structure, the services and how to request them, the policies, standards, success stories, dashboards, etc. Examples of these channels include intranet portals, email, magazines, newsletters, etc.

Customer Relationship: In many enterprises, the easy part is to make new customers. The hard part is maintaining a relationship with existing customers and creating loyalty. One result of a successful Data Governance implementation is that people will appreciate the Data Governance team's value. Customers with a great experience and tangible benefits will recommend the work of this team. In the Customer Relationship section of the canvas, identify the means for keeping customers' interest. For instance, notifying about updates to data sources, offering support to identifying and document business terms, training, and so on.

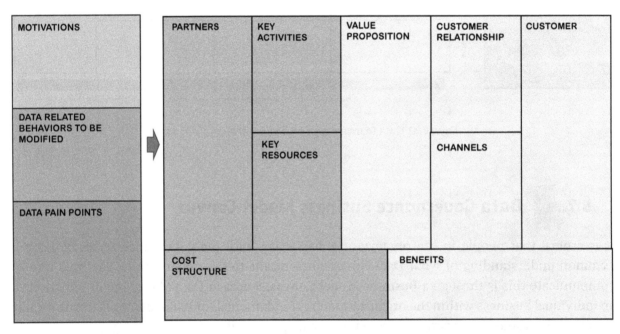

Figure 22 Data Governance Business Model Canvas

Benefits: It is essential to express the benefits of Data Governance to the organization in business terms. Adding quantitative elements is great when possible but not mandatory. As the operation matures, include figures of quantitative benefits in updated versions of this Canvas.

Partners: Deploying and executing Data Governance requires support and collaboration from diverse areas in the organization. One clear example is the Project Management Office. Because all the projects go through this office, it can mandate activities to improve Data Management, like documenting Metadata and enforcing requirements through the project's budget. Another important partner is the IT solution design team or architecture team. Solution architects can be trained to identify the lack of data standards and to guide the project leads to adhere to standards.

Key Activities: It is not uncommon to hear Data Governance teams complain about having to do very diverse data-related activities but not Data Governance. This is mainly derived from the lack of understanding of Data Governance. And this is precisely the purpose of this canvas. Therefore, the canvas is the right place to list the core activities the Data Governance team will focus on. Listing them here will prevent the organization from throwing all data activities to the Data Governance team. Examples include producing policies and managing data sources inventory, the business glossary, and the data quality process (often, conditions do not allow for a separate team for Data Quality, and the Data Governance team must initially launch it). There are no right and wrong key activities. This canvas aims to communicate what we expect the team to do.

Key Resources: Once the key activities are listed, we identify the resources required to execute them. Here we need to record not only human resources but also material ones in the form of infrastructure, licenses, platforms, equipment, etc.

Cost Structure: This section helps create awareness of the costs of having Data Governance. We drive the information in the Cost Structure section from the Key Resources. It is essential to indicate one-time and recurring costs. If quantitative information is unavailable, this list can include topics to be accounted for.

5.8.   Key Concepts

Data Strategy Canvases are a means to communicate the different levels of Data Strategy in a synthesized way, such that each Data Strategy can be described in a single slide.

5.9.   Things to Keep in Mind

1.   The power of Canvas resides in its ability to communicate several related ideas on a single slide that can be clearly understood by different audiences.

2.   Each Data Strategy Canvas has a specific purpose and is related to the rest of the Data Strategy Canvases. Collectively they tell a complete story about what will happen in Data Management.

3.   Data Strategy Canvases help to set expectations across the organization about how Data Management will bring value to the organization.

5.10.   Interview on Data Strategy

EXPERT INTERVIEWED: Tom Redman[39]

Tom Redman, better known as the "Data Doc," is an internationally recognized expert in Data Quality and author of several titles in this area. He's co-author of the Leaders Data Manifesto. He has helped leaders and companies understand their most important issues and opportunities in the data space, chart a course, and build the organizational capabilities they need to execute. From start-ups to enormous multinationals, from senior executives and Chief Data Officers to people in the middle struggling to get something started, he helps build Data Driven futures. To do so, he combines a visionary's perspective on the data landscape with deep expertise in analytics and data quality.

Given your vast experience as a consultant in Data Quality, how often do you find a well-defined horizontal Data Strategy guiding the data-related work and responding to business strategy in your customers' organizations?

So far, I have not found a Data Strategy that meets the criteria you laid out. Let me provide some background. In my view, the fundamental "strategy" question is, "How do we aim to compete in the marketplace?" "Data Strategy" and "business strategy" must be inseparable in answering the question.

Second, I don't think companies should think much about strategy until they get the basics in place. A good strategy must be achievable and, until they have the basics in place, companies have no way of speculating on what they can achieve. I've seen too many starry-eyed plans that couldn't pass the "achievable test."

Finally, I know a lot of data people are trying to align their work to business strategy. Great, but not sufficient. Businesspeople should also be asking themselves how they can create a competitive advantage from data.

What do you think is the role of Data Strategy in the success or failure of a Data Driven Transformation initiative?

I can't imagine you can transform anything without a solid data plan.

But just to be clear, I'm very skeptical that many initiatives I see labeled "transformation" have much chance. Transformation is hard—it requires a range of talent, a sense of urgency of urgency, a very compelling vision, and courage. I'm just not seeing companies assembling these things. Too much talk, too little hard work.

---

[39] Tom Redman https://www.linkedin.com/in/tomredman/

From your perspective, who do you think should drive the creation and maintenance of a Data Strategy, and which stakeholders need to participate in this process?

The people who have the most to gain should drive the creation of Data Strategy. Data professionals have much to gain, but usually not nearly as much as businesspeople. I know of one CDO who is leading the charge, but they are putting the basics in place—perhaps the company will be ready for a strategy in another year.

So generally, the business should drive. Data people can work behind the scenes, perhaps even in partnership, but most often, there must be business leadership.

Two other things: You didn't ask about execution, but that is key. And most of the resources lie in the business—further compelling the need for business leadership. Second, I've already noted that few companies are ready for an enterprise-wide Data Strategy. For now, though, I encourage individual units, even down to the team level, to set and pursue very aggressive strategies. Companies learn by doing.

How would you recommend a new Data Governance lead create awareness and get buy-in from Senior Management on the relevance of building an integral and horizontal Data Strategy as the foundation for a successful Data Management program?

I want to be a little cautious here. I find that too many data professionals want senior leaders to "understand data." Then they (senior management) will really be able to help. But it is a fool's errand. I've been knee-deep in all things data for a very long time, and I feel I'm only beginning to understand data. How can a senior executive, spending just a few minutes on the topic, truly understand data?

Instead, data professionals should think much more about the help they really need from senior leaders. I've seen data professionals try to get senior leaders to sign off on arcane business rules. Senior leaders know nothing about these, can't really help, and quickly get turned off. Further, this is not what the data program needs.

I find almost all senior management wants to help—most simply view doing so as their job. It is best to ask them for things you really need. For example, one client of mine needed to build a network of embedded data managers. So, she clarified exactly what she wanted and why and made a specific request. Of course, it was granted. Another asked a senior leader to make fifteen minutes for data during a townhall meeting and to speak from the heart on how he viewed data fitting into the Division's mission. This leader did a better job than this person could have imagined.

In summary, data professionals should NOT ask senior leaders to do their jobs for them. But they should ask senior leaders for help where they need it, with it and with organizational capability. They should make their requests as specific as possible.

6. The Journey: Path to an Effective Data Management Program

The journey matters as much as the goal.

Kalpana Chawla

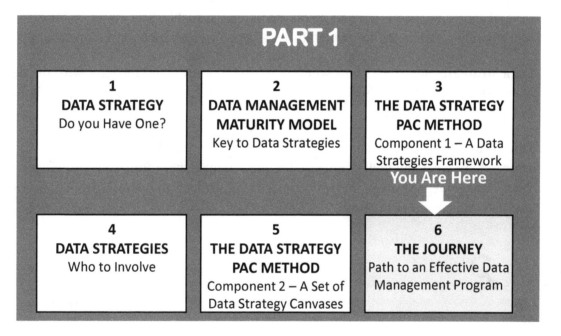

Whenever I finish teaching a Data Management 101 course, I hear recurrent questions: "Where should we begin?" "Should all the Data Management functions be addressed simultaneously?" "What are the success factors for a Data Management Program?" I usually respond by showing them the map in Figure 23 with four zones to go through to produce an effective Data Management program. These include:

1. Educating the organization on Data Management fundamentals and defining a standing training program

2. Assessing Data Management maturity

3. Developing Data Strategies to prioritize data work

4. Designing Operating Models, starting with Data Governance and Data Quality.

This chapter describes the journey depicted through these four topics (again, Figure 23).

Picture the moment you use a map application to find out how to get to your destination. The application will show you different options to get to the same place. Some options may include a toll road. Others may not have tolls but can take longer. The map in Figure 23 shows four areas or zones we must go through to get to our destination: the Data Management Program.

- **Education**: The first zone is Education, as we start by spreading basic data concepts across the organization. This will contribute to building a common data language and understanding of concepts, roles, techniques, and metrics of Data Management. There could be different ways to transit this zone: webinars, formal training, short videos, etc.

- **Assessment**: The Data Management Maturity Assessment represents the second zone. Here, the view lets you understand where the organization fits in this area. There are several routes to follow, depending on the budget available. The Maturity Model I am more familiar with is DCAM, which I find as a robust approach, based on capabilities.

- **Data Strategies**: Once we know where the organization is and the gaps with the desired state, we can go into the third zone, the Data Strategies, where the strategies discussed in Chapter 3 are defined.

- **Operations**: When we leave the Data Strategy zone, we go into the Operating Models zone, where we detail how to operate the Data Management functions prioritized in the Data Management Strategy. In this zone, we can produce an operational plan or a set for the Data Management Program.

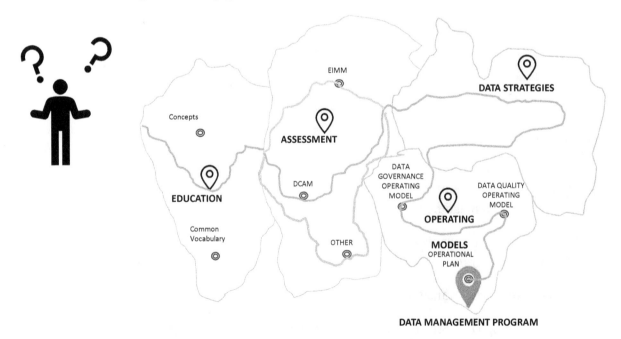

Figure 23 Route to get to an effective Data Management Program

6.1.   Education

Data Literacy has become one of the most important buzzwords over the last few years. Data Literacy is the absolute foundation for developing a data culture.

Data Literacy is the ability to read, analyze, work, and communicate with data (Data Literacy Project, 2021). It is now so critical to companies that it has been hailed as the second language of business. The increasingly pervasive nature of data makes it crucial for all employees to learn to "speak data." (Gartner Group, 2018)

Laura Sebastian-Coleman describes building Data Literacy as part of the People Challenge, one of the five challenges of Data Quality Management. She compares Data Literacy with any literacy:

Any kind of literacy can be understood as a combination of knowledge, skills, and experience. Literacy begins when a person learns the alphabet and recognizes how words are represented in written form. It develops through an explicit knowledge of the structure of written language – sentences, paragraphs, and chapters. More importantly, as a reader reads more, he or she begins to understand nuances in texts. Experience reading literature hones skills in seeing connections, understanding structure, and recognizing how an author's choices in revealing information enrich the experience of the story. Experience reading nonfiction, science, history, and even technical information has similar effects as all of these require a person to abstract information and understand it from different perspectives. Reading data requires similar knowledge and skills. Knowledge is gained, and skills are honed through the experience of using and thereby interpreting data. (Sebastian-Coleman, 2022).

Thus, developing Data Literacy across an organization is a continuous process. We must consider many aspects, ranging from the knowledge of data to the experience gained by working with data. Laura Sebastian-Coleman groups all the Data Literacy components into three main general Literacy Components: Knowledge, Skills, and Experience.

Educating on the fundamentals of Data Management, like teaching the alphabet, will allow people to develop skills to apply in gaining experience in any of the Data Management functions. It is like the essential building blocks to building a data culture and developing Data Literacy.

To govern and manage data, there must be a data education program. One that recognizes the educational and training needs of people around the organization based on their role and exposure to data. Not everyone requires the same level of training, but everyone needs to know the alphabet: the basic core concepts of Data Management. It is impressive how much misunderstanding about Data Management I find every time I start a class, even when many students have been working with data for a while. A few specialized professionals will require training to certify their knowledge and experience.

To go through this first zone, start by defining a combination of different media to reach the widest audience in the organization to communicate the essential concepts of Data Management. These could include an executive talk performed in different time slots and recorded and published on the intranet. We can integrate data education into a corporate educational program to make it mandatory. Then complement these with "data capsules" broadcasted as part of an articulated program coordinated with the internal Communication team.

The next level of training on Data Management fundamentals includes teaching about Data Management. For example, what each Data Management function is and how it relates to the rest of the functions and to business goals. Even for people who have dedicated several years to working in a specific function, like Data Integration or Data Operations, it becomes essential to understand how other areas must interact to manage data effectively. Learning the fundamentals of Data Management typically motivates people to learn more or to get more deeply involved in a specific function to develop skills and get experience.

The educational or training events could be beneficial when business and IT audiences mix as they can also learn from other's perspectives. An additional benefit is that the training sessions can help with identifying key stakeholders needed to participate in the Data Management Maturity Assessment and the Data Strategies definition.

6.2. Assessment

Chapter 2 discussed the benefits of using a capability-based Data Management Maturity Model when defining the Data Management Strategy. We also reviewed the most recognized models. We now meet this topic again as the second zone in our journey where we need to understand where the organization stands concerning Data Management functions.

I frequently hear from organization leaders that they are just starting a Data Management Program, so they think they don't need an assessment. They assume the organization is at the first maturity level. Nevertheless, understanding how stakeholders from different parts of the organization see the organization and comparing this perception against a reference model helps to identify motivations that serve as inputs to the Data Strategies. The gaps identified will help with prioritization in each phase of the strategy definition.

Whatever Maturity Model is adopted, the key to success is to engage core stakeholders from across the organization in the evaluation. Collaboration is key. And the maturity assessment is another excellent opportunity to identify participants to define the Data Strategies.

6.3. Data Strategies

We reach the Data Strategies zone after performing the Data Management Maturity Assessment. In Chapter 3, we discussed the Data Strategies Framework and identified the types of Data Strategies required. The fundamental Data Strategies to define in the first stage are the Data

Alignment Strategy, The Data Management Strategy, and the Data Governance Strategy. The order and pace at which we produce the Data Management Function Strategies depend on their prioritization in the Data Management Strategy.

In Chapter 4, we emphasized the importance of engaging stakeholders in defining Data Strategies. Organizational unit leaders will identify these individuals during the educational and assessment sessions.

Chapter 7, The Data Strategy PAC Method: Component 3 – Data Strategy Cycle, describes what happens in this third zone of the journey so that I won't go deeper into this here. It's worth mentioning that once you prioritize goals through the Data Management and Data Governance strategies (Chapter 3), it is straightforward to derive an annual roadmap to use in managing expectations. Together, these three provide critical input to the Operating Models.

6.4.   Operating Models

In the last zone of our journey toward a comprehensive Data Management program, we develop conceptual designs of the operating models for the top priority Data Management functions (as identified in the Data Management Strategy). Data Governance is always the priority. There are different considerations to designing such a model. For example:

- David Plotkin provides a complete study of data stewardship, which he defines as "the operational aspect of an overall Data Governance program – where the actual day-to-day work of governing an enterprise's data gets done" (Plotkin, 2021).

- Robert Seiner advocates for Non-Invasive Data Governance, "where a less intrusive but more effective Data Governance can be very helpful. You may want to ramp up your Data Governance model by leveraging other governance structures already in the organization" (Seiner, 2014).

- You can complement this approach with the diplomatic and no-coercive approach of Håkan Edvinsson: "The Diplomacy approach strives to reduce the formalities and remove the coercive parts of traditional Data Governance" (Edvinsson H. , 2020).

You can use these references to determine what components will be part of the model (e.g., stewardship, standing committees, working groups, policies) and how they will work together (e.g., collaboration principles, decision-making, level of formality). Remember, the goal is to design your organization's best Data Governance Operating Model. It is fundamental to consider your organizational culture (how new ideas and processes are received, how decisions are taken, how change is managed, etc.). It is also essential to consider the available resources to operate the model. The conceptual design must address current and future needs, and it should work for an incremental deployment across the organization.

Once the Operating Models for Data Governance and the prioritized Data Management Functions (Data Quality, Data Architecture, Data Security, etc.) are defined, it is time to design an operational plan. This detailed plan will derive from the high-level roadmap. The Data Management program, our destination in this journey, is a multi-year program. It will require an operational plan for each year. With the plans defined, we enter a cycle of execution and control to implement the models and execute the plans.

In many organizations, teams launch Data Governance without clear direction. Then they pretend to govern all the data in the organization. In other words, they find shortcuts and try to skip to the end of the process without passing through the zones I described. In most cases, the result is that the Data Governance team gets lost. Once lost, they come easily to a point where they don't know which path to follow.

6.5.   Key Concepts

The Data Management Journey describes the path an organization takes to build a Data Management Program. It starts by educating the organization and fostering a common language in data. It continues by doing the assessment of Data Management Maturity, defining Data Strategies, and implementing a Data Governance Operating Model and an Operational Plan.

6.6.   Things to Keep in Mind

1.   A data educational program must be in place to provide the level of training needed for each role exposed to data in the organization.

2.   Training on the ABCs of Data Management and Data Management Maturity Assessment sessions can be good forums through which to identify key stakeholders for the definition of Data Strategies.

3.   Annual roadmaps can be derived from the Data Management and Data Governance Strategies and become the input to the Data Management Program's Operational Plans.

6.7.   Interview on Data Strategy

EXPERT INTERVIEWED: David Plotkin[40]

David Plotkin is a Data Governance and Data Quality manager with expertise in Data Architecture, data marts, logical and physical Data Modeling, database design, business requirements and business rules, Metadata Management, Data Quality, profiling, data integrity, and Data Stewardship. Experience in the fields of Financial Services (at large banks and wealth management companies), Energy/Engineering, Healthcare, Human Resources, Insurance, Education (K-12) and Retail. Sought-after speaker for DAMA, Data Governance, and University conferences. Expert at working with IT teams on implementation of large systems with complex processes, he is the author of the book *Data Stewardship*, and presenter for a 2-day course on the implementation of Data Stewardship.

Given your vast experience as a Data Management professional and specifically as a Stewardship and Metadata Management promoter in the corporate world, how often have you found senior management commitment to producing a well-defined horizontal Data Strategy guiding the data-related work and responding to business strategy in the organizations you have collaborated with?

Senior management often seems to be resistant to implementing a well-defined Data Strategy to guide the data-related work and respond to business strategy. In cases where there is an urgent need for a specific data-related "solution" (such as Master Data Management, Reference Data, Data Governance, or improving data quality), creating a Data Strategy first is often viewed as a waste of time. Of course, it is NOT a waste of time since a Data Strategy provides the guidance and infrastructure from which tactical decisions can and should be made. Also affecting the willingness to create a Data Strategy as a first step is the perception that it takes many months to get to a robust strategy, and meanwhile the other urgent work is on hold.

The key to overcoming this resistance is to convince senior management that the Data Strategy can be quickly constructed if it is initially just a framework, which guides the other work and gets filled out as other work is done, and more is learned. It is an error to think of a Data Strategy as "fixed" and unchanging, instead, it should be flexible so that it can be changed as the business strategy becomes better understood.

What do you think is the role of Data Strategy in the success or failure of a Data Driven Transformation initiative?

A Data Strategy is an important part of a Data Driven transformation initiative, and directly contributes to the success of such an effort. The Data Driven transformation affects the business

---

[40] David Plotkin https://www.linkedin.com/in/davidnplotkin/

model, processes, and even organizational culture. Underlying all these changes are enormous amounts of data. In fact, the very heart of a Data Driven transformation (as you can tell from the name!) is that decisions the business makes in response to changing conditions, actions of competitors and regulatory agencies, and process changes, are data driven. Thus, proper management of data is crucial. A Data Strategy guides how the enterprise manages data and Metadata – how it governs that data, decides what data to use, whether (and how) to improve the quality of the data so it can be used, and how to transform and streamline the use of the data to meet business goals. Without a Data Strategy, a digital transformation is likely to be less effective and may even fail completely.

From your perspective, who do you think should drive the creation and maintenance of a Data Strategy, and which stakeholders need to participate in this process?

One of the more obvious answers to "who should drive the creation and maintenance of a Data Strategy" would be Enterprise Architecture. But whether they are a good choice depends on the culture at the company. While Enterprise Architecture is often known for CREATING strategies, they are often (though not always) not very good at implementing those strategies for business advantage. That is, if the created strategy is not practical, does not consider the business imperatives, or requires leadership and expertise that the enterprise architects lack, it may prove useless. I have found that it can be difficult to find an Enterprise Architect who is good at creating AND executing strategies, including finding the stakeholders in the business, executive support, convincing the business to participate because of the value added, and guiding it to a finished product – including designating the tactics needed to execute on the strategy.

Another possibility is a combination of experienced Data Management professionals, such as the leads for major data initiatives such Data Governance, Master Data Management, Data Warehouse / Data Lake, Metadata Management, and Data Quality. Guided by someone who knows how to construct a Data Strategy, these subject matter experts can work together to ensure that the Data Strategy contains all the components that would be required to execute on these crucial areas. In addition, each of these components has its own stakeholders that are driving the execution, and who can provide business input on what business goals are most important.

How would you recommend a new Data Governance lead create awareness and get buy-in from Senior Management on the relevance of building an integral and horizontal Data Strategy as the foundation for a successful Data Management program?

I would recommend that a new Data Governance lead team up with the sorts of people that I mentioned above, to participate in creating awareness and buy-in from Senior Management. That said, I don't think that a new Data Governance lead should be focusing on this, but instead be supporting it. Data Governance practitioners / leads have a tremendous amount to do and are not necessarily experts in building and "selling" data strategies – that is not what they were hired for. They should support the effort because Data Governance both contributes to and benefits from a solid Data Strategy.

PART 2

Implementing the Method

Part 1 explained the first two components of **The Data Strategy PAC Method**: the Data Strategies Framework and the Set of Data Strategy Canvases. Part 2 details the third component of the Method: The Data Strategy Cycle. If you skipped Part 1, reference previous chapters to get a better understanding as you apply the ten steps in the Data Strategy Cycle.

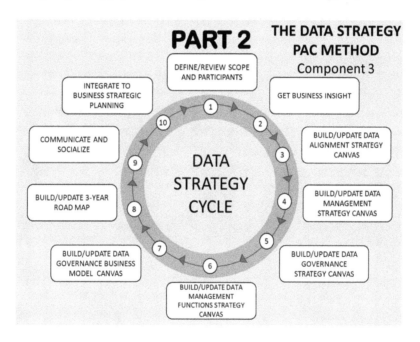

Figure 24 Ten Steps of Data Strategy Cycle

7. The Data Strategy PAC Method: Component 3 - Data Strategy Cycle

---

It is common sense to take a method and try it. If it fails, admit it frankly and try another. But above all, try something.

Franklin D. Roosevelt

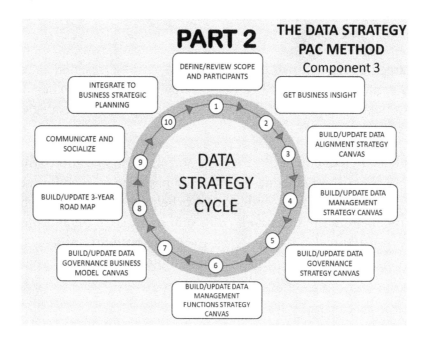

7.1.   Introduction to the Data Strategy Ten Step Cycle[41]

It is time to go through the ten steps of the **Data Strategy Cycle**, the third component of **The Data Strategy PAC Method**. If you have read the previous six chapters, you have all the context you need to understand the Method. You know where it came from and why it was defined. If you start directly with the methodology, you will find references to previous

---

[41] Inspired in Danette McGilvray's TEN STEPS to Quality Data and Trusted Information ™ http://www.gfalls.com/

109

chapters as you read through the steps in the cycle. These will direct you to detail and additional context.

PAC stands for **P**ragmatic, **A**gile, and **C**ommunicable (using its meaning of communicating ideas).[42] Figure 25 shows its three components again:

1. **A Data Strategies Framework:** This represents why we need a set of tightly interlocked Data Strategies rather than one. This framework traces the business strategy to the milestones in a Data Governance Roadmap and, from there, to the Data Governance Operational Plan. See Chapter 3.

2. **A set of Data Strategy Canvases:** These describe the Data Strategies. A canvas is a concept for representing a set of ideas on a single slide (simulating the canvas an artist uses when doing a painting). In our case, the canvases represent the strategies included in the Data Strategies Framework. This concept was inspired by the *Business Model Canvas,* by Alexander Osterwalder et al.[43] See Chapter 5 for a detailed description of each canvas.

3. **A Data Strategy Cycle:** Consists of ten steps that must be repeated annually in the enterprise's strategic planning to keep the strategies connected to business goals. (Following annual cycles does not preclude revisiting the Data Strategies within a cycle if a business strategy changes.)

The method's simplicity makes it effective for large and small organizations; the only difference will be the number of people participating. The method has even worked for me as an individual consultant when I have used it in my own business. It helps me understand what I must do and for whom, so I can communicate effectively with others. In large organizations, stakeholders representing each organizational unit must define the Data Strategy Canvases. This makes a Data Strategy holistic (considering all the organizational units' needs) and open, as discussed in Chapter 3.

---

[42] https://dictionary.cambridge.org/dictionary/english-spanish/communicable

[43] Alexander Osterwalder https://www.alexosterwalder.com/ Business Model Canvas https://bit.ly/3LSV4bb

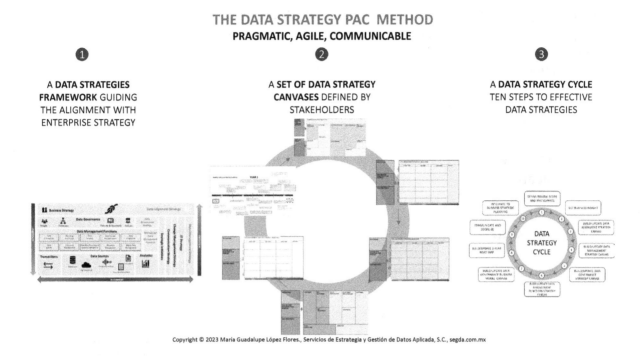

Figure 25 Components of The Data Strategy PAC Method

Figure 26 indicates the order in which we define the different Data Strategies.

1. **Data Alignment Strategy**: This strategy responds to the enterprise's strategic objectives, data requirements, and data-related pain points. To define this strategy, we identify and prioritize these inputs.

2. **Data Management Strategy**: Using the Data Alignment Strategy as input, this strategy prioritizes the Data Management Functions to be set up or matured (at the center of the Framework), as well as the organizational units and the data domains where the functions will be applied.

3. **Data Governance Strategy**: This strategy prioritizes the Data Governance capabilities to establish and the objects (processes, reports, data domains, data sources, data repositories, etc.) to govern.

4. **Specific Data Management Function Strategy**: Each Data Management Function prioritized in the Data Management Strategy must have its strategy.

Figure 24 illustrates the steps to produce the Data Strategies. In this chapter, we will explore each of these steps. Before executing the steps, get buy-in from Senior Management. While almost everyone will say having a Data Strategy and improving information quality are important, there is usually pushback about dedicating time and money to work on these things. Pushback may sound something like this:

- We already have a Data Strategy...we are moving our data to the cloud.

- Having a Data Strategy is a good idea, but it's too expensive and takes months to produce. We are in urgent need of putting Master Data in place.

- The operation can't stop. We cannot dedicate people to write a Data Strategy. Let's have someone write it for us.

- Data Strategy is worthless. We've been operating for years without one.

- Data Strategy is not practical. What we need is immediate solutions to our data problems.

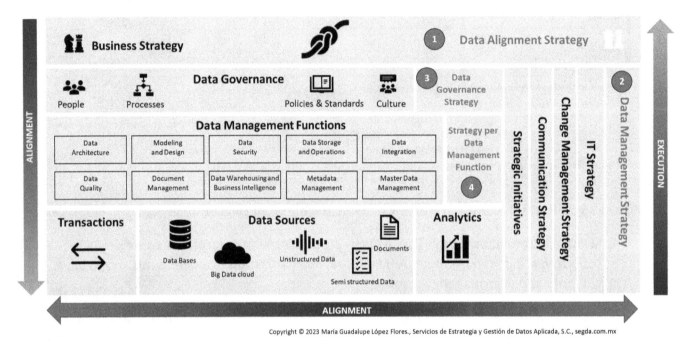

Figure 26 Order to Produce Data Strategies

Before asking for buy-in, prepare yourself to refute those arguments with ideas like these:

- **Holistic**: For effective results, Data Strategy must go beyond how to evolve technical platforms and solutions. It must holistically address business needs, motivations, data-related pain points, undesirable data-related behaviors, and, most importantly, business strategic objectives. It also must be an open strategy; stakeholders from all over the organization must contribute to it and participate in its definition. This will give them reasons to support its execution. Finally, it must be easy for everyone in the organization to find and understand.

- **Planned**: Prepare a timeline that clarifies how long it will take to develop the first iteration of the Data Strategies. Producing The Data Alignment Strategy, The Data Management Strategy, and The Data Governance Strategy. For the first time, we can complete the Data Governance Business Model and Data Governance Roadmap in nine weeks.

- **Open/Inclusive**: For large organizations, if a single person or a consultant defines the Data Strategy, it will be hard to execute, as most stakeholders will identify with the strategy only if they have been involved in its definition. Include stakeholders from across the organization.

- **Support with Evidence**: Document a case where the organization invested in technology platforms or solutions to remediate data without having the expected outcome.

- **Communicable**: Prepare a one-pager with the Data Strategy Charter to communicate the practical approach, the timeline, the resources required, and the expected benefit.

Defining Data Strategies must not be an isolated effort to support IT initiatives and data operations. Integrate the process into the organization's annual strategic planning. This cycle closes when you embed Data Strategies in strategic business planning.

Before going into the Data Strategy Cycle, define all the steps as if you are doing this for the first time. Data Strategies, once defined, are living documents that must be updated if there are changes in the Enterprise Strategy. Revisit and update the Data Strategies defined here at least once a year using the ten steps described here. This annual review takes significantly less time as the organization begins to execute it with maturity; because, not surprisingly, modifying an existing canvas is always to be easier than starting one from scratch.

7.2.   Following the Data Strategy Cycle

7.2.1 Step 1: Define/Review Scope, Participants, and Resources

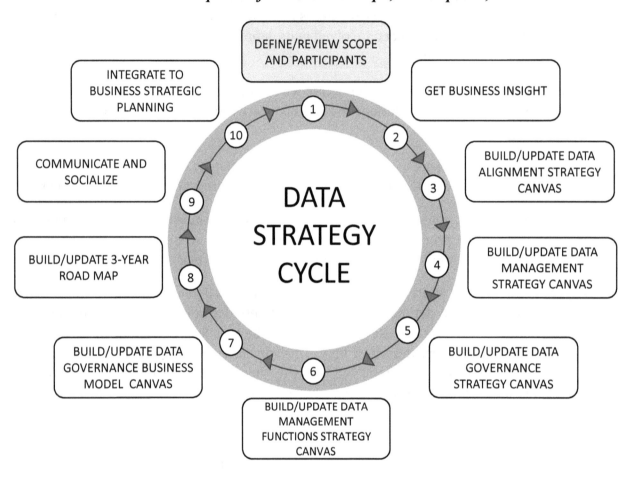

This first step focuses on identifying the stakeholders who will define the Data Strategies. The holistic approach requires stakeholders from across the organization. For large organizations, especially multinational corporations, define the scope of this initiative at this point. Will the initiative start at the corporate level and be cascaded to business units? Or will it be a local initiative having corporate definitions as input? We first need a Data Strategy sponsor with a strong organizational influence to determine the best approach. This person should make the scope proposal and get the buy-in from top management.

Since multiple stakeholders will participate, you must carefully propose a schedule that fits their agendas and the organization's timeframes.

Step 1 Process Flow

1. **Have a Data Strategy Sponsor:** Your sponsor can be from either the Business or IT. The most important characteristics of the sponsor are that he/she is committed to having a

holistic, open Data Strategy and that he/she can influence others in top management regarding funding, collaboration, and stakeholder engagement.

2. **Define Scope and Identify Participants**: The intent is to have as many organizational units represented as possible. There is no rule about the level the stakeholders have within the organization – the group may include both senior management and operational people. All should know the processes and data-related problems in their units. And they need to speak up and not feel intimidated when senior management is in the room.

3. **Have a One-page Data Strategy Charter**: The one-pager must focus on the essential information: **what** is proposed, **why** it is proposed, **how** it will be implemented, **who** is required to participate, **when** it will be achieved, and its **benefits**. Include supporting slides to communicate the Data Strategy initiative, attendees' profiles, and time required from them.

4. **Have a Robust and Engaging Message**: Prepare a powerful message to share with people at all levels across the organization. Have your sponsor record a short (three-to-five-minute) video focused on the message. Use this to open your working meetings when you meet an audience for the first time and engage stakeholders in this initiative. Sponsors are generally within the top management, with very complicated agendas. Recording the message enables the sponsor to provide ongoing support without adding drag to timelines.

5. **Decide on a Workshop Format**: We can do the work in workshops or online meetings. The second option allows the participation of people in different locations. Decide this and arrange the corresponding facilities.

6. **Decide the Techniques and Tools to be Used**: Design Thinking techniques, introduced by Hebert Simon in 1969 in his *The Sciences of the Artificial*, now in its third edition (Simon, 2019), are very effective for this work.[44] These techniques allow us to collect the information we need to define Data Strategies in a way that creates an empathetic environment. For on-site meetings, the "Brown Paper" technique works very well. You cover the meeting room's walls with brown paper on which you can draw boxes for inputs (Questions, Motivations, Business Strategic Objectives, Behaviors, Pain Points) or different canvases depending on the session. Participants move around the room and provide content on post-its. Some offices have meeting rooms with glass walls that work well for this technique. Similar dynamics can be achieved through collaborative tools when the meeting is virtual. Participants can share their ideas, and then each

---

[44] Design Thinking https://www.interaction-design.org/literature/topics/design-thinking

participant will see the whole set of ideas and vote on the top 10. When selecting your tool, make sure it has the capability for voting.

7. **Schedule the Workshops**: The objective is to have as many stakeholders as possible actively participating. Therefore, choosing the best days and times for the meetings is essential. Plan a schedule for all the meetings required for steps 2-8. Ensure the audience receives invitations at least two weeks in advance. Avoid overlapping with critical dates in the organization, like the end of the month.

8. **Define a Clear and Engaging Message for the Invitation**: Carefully craft the meeting invitation from the subject to the content. If possible, arrange for it to be sent from the sponsor or another person whom participants are likely to pay attention.

9. **Ensure Timeliness**: Send invitations at least two weeks before the event, followed by reminders to keep the event on the radar.

Considerations for Small Business/Organization: Similar steps apply to small organizations where there may be a smaller number of stakeholders. In smaller organizations, a single person may play several roles.

Table 3 Step 1 Summary

Step 1. Define/Review the Scope and Participants	
Objective	<ul><li>Based on the defined scope. Identify the organizational units that must be represented in the definition/review of Data Strategies.</li><li>Identify individual stakeholders to participate in the Data Strategy workshops.</li><li>Organize agendas so participants know what to expect.</li><li>Schedule workshops, ensuring you avoid major conflicts.</li><li>Manage logistics and readiness checklist to assure participants' attendance, as well as the availability of facilities and tools.</li></ul>
Purpose	<ul><li>Ensure conditions are set to produce a holistic Data Strategy with the participation of key stakeholders representing the whole organization.</li><li>Ensure the sponsor sends a strong message to participant areas.</li><li>Ensure that organizational units that use or have an impact on data can influence the Data Strategies.</li><li>Ensure engagement from all selected organizational units.</li><li>Make the best use of people's time by ensuring participants in the Data Strategies workshop meetings have a strong knowledge of the processes in their units and the type of existing data-related problems.</li><li>Ensure everything is ready to start running the Data Strategy definition workshops.</li></ul>

Step 1. Define/Review the Scope and Participants	
Inputs	<ul><li>Scope definition (corporation/company/country/subsidiaries)</li><li>Organizational charts</li><li>Existing governance bodies</li></ul>
Techniques and Tools	<ul><li>Data Strategies Stakeholders Pyramid (Figure 15)</li><li>Facilitation Questionnaire</li><li>Data Strategy Charter</li><li>Readiness Checklist</li></ul>
Outputs	<ul><li>Data Strategy Charter</li><li>Readiness Checklist</li><li>List of organizational units included in the process.</li><li>List of participants, including their organizational units, roles, and workshop meetings they need to attend.</li><li>Calendar of workshops, agendas, and message to invite participants.</li><li>Recording of the sponsor's engaging message</li></ul>
Participants	<ul><li>Data Governance Lead or equivalent</li><li>Data Strategy sponsor</li><li>Governance Body that includes the most relevant leading managers</li></ul>
Checkpoint	<ul><li>Have a Data Strategy sponsor.</li><li>Define scope and participants.</li><li>Have a one-pager Data Strategy Charter.</li><li>Ensure the sponsor records a strong and engaging message.</li><li>Decide workshop format.</li><li>Decide the techniques and tools to use.</li><li>Define the best schedule for the workshops.</li><li>Define a clear and engaging message for the invites.</li><li>Send invitations at least two weeks in advance.</li><li>Ensure invitations get confirmed.</li></ul>

7.2.2 Step 2: Get Business Insight

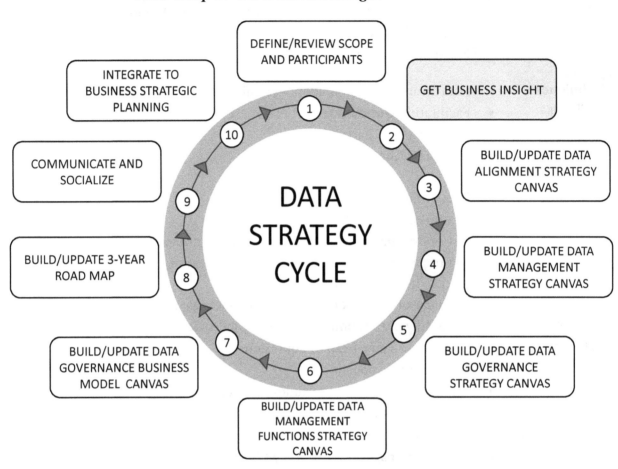

Dedicate the second step to understanding the organization. Ideally, it starts by reviewing the Enterprise Strategy. Sometimes, this strategy is not documented. When it is, it is not necessarily understood in the same way across the organization. This step aims to get consensus on the top business strategic objectives as the primary input to produce the Data Strategies.

In Chapter 5, we discussed other inputs to the definition of Data Strategies:

- Business Questions

- Data-related Pain Points

- Motivations

- Behaviors to be changed

- Strategic Initiatives

The goals of this step are to both identify and prioritize these inputs in the interest of the overall organization, not just the individual business units. Doing so requires the active participation of all the stakeholders identified in Step 1.

This is the first encounter with organizational stakeholders, where a mix of top management, Directors, and operational subject matter experts come together, all with very tight agendas and jealous of their time, so you can expect skepticism in the meeting. This is why it is essential to start with a concise introduction explaining why you invited them and what you expect from the group.

Step 2 Process Flow

1. **Gather the Latest Business Strategic Objectives**: This task includes gathering contextual information to expedite Data Strategies' definition. In a medium or large organization, the Planning Area team may be your first touch point for business objectives. Or objectives may be included in an Enterprise Strategy, typically documented with a five-year horizon and updated annually. If you are lucky, management may have published this strategy on the organization's intranet. Finding documented information about more than the business objectives and motivations may be difficult. You will gather most of the additional information during the Business Insight Workshops.

2. **Prepare your Tools**: Before running the workshop meetings, you must prepare your Design Thinking tools for each activity. Create templates that allow attendees to fill in their ideas. Have some baseline items or examples for each topic to start discussions and illustrate your request. Populate this content in the tool before the sessions to expedite the activities during the meetings:

   a) **Business Strategic Objectives:** Based on what you found as the context in point 1, create a list of all the Business Strategic Objectives. During the Business Insight Workshop, ask the attendees to add objectives to the list if something is missing and to prioritize the top three to five objectives if not yet prioritized.

   b) **Business Questions:** Ask all attendees to list the business questions they ask to run their business. This is difficult, as different people will interpret the idea of a "business question" differently. The best way to clarify it is to present three to five example questions in the template where participants will drop their questions.

   c) **Data Management Motivations:** Ask participants to express their motivations for embarking on or enhancing the Data Management program. Based on what you have learned about the organization, identify three motivations for the Data Management program and add them to the template where participants will drop their motivations.

    d) **Data Pain Points**: The fourth activity will be to list all the data-related pain points, so again, prepare the template. Ultimately, all participants must vote on the top ten pain points.

    e) **Prioritize Behaviors to be Changed**: The last activity of this section is to identify and prioritize undesirable behaviors related to data that need to be changed. For this activity, prepare a place for a simple list. You may want to draft some examples (e.g., Reports designers not indicating the data source used in their reports). Once you create the list with the participants' ideas, ask them to vote for the top five.

3. **Schedule the Workshops**: Because people have busy schedules, it is important to send out meeting invitations for all the workshop sessions well ahead of time – at least two weeks before the kick-off meeting, so that people block their calendars.

4. **Conduct the Workshops**: Workshops must be agile. This is why preparation is essential. Use a timekeeper. The first sessions have the following goals:

    a) **Prioritize the Top Three Business Strategic Objectives**: Using the template with the draft content produced in (2. a), attendees should add to the list if required. After this, get the group to agree on the priority of the objectives.

    b) **Prioritize Business Questions**: Ask all attendees to list the questions they ask to run their business. Use the template with drafted content produced in (2. b). Ask all the participants to vote on the top 10 questions relevant to the whole organization.

    c) **Prioritize Data Management Motivations**: Ask participants to express their motivations for embarking on or enhancing the Data Management program. Ask them to vote on the top five.

    d) **Prioritize Data Pain Points**: Ask participants to list the data-related pain points. They may start with issues related to the infrastructure, like not having enough capacity or high response times. You may need to guide them to identify problems related to the data itself, such as inconsistent reports due to poor quality data. Participants must vote on the top ten pain points.

    e) **Prioritize Behaviors to be Changed**: The last input to identify and prioritize is represented by the undesirable behaviors related to data that need to be changed. The examples you prepare for this activity will help guide the audience. Once you create the list with the ideas of all the participants, ask them to vote for the top five.

    f) **Identify and Prioritize Strategic Initiatives**: One additional element to consider in the Data Management and the Data Governance strategies is the prioritized list of ongoing or close to get started programs or projects with the highest priority in the organization to support meeting the business strategic objectives. These initiatives are the best candidates to benefit from the Data Management practice.

Table 4 Step 2 Summary

Step 2. Get Business Insight	
Objective	• Identify current business strategic objectives • Identify key business questions that lead to decision making • Identify all the business drivers and motivations for defining or enhancing a Data Management Program • Identify all currently ongoing strategic initiatives in the organization • Identify data-related pain points in the organization • Identify undesirable data-related behaviors
Purpose	• Collect all the inputs required to define the Data Strategies • Prioritize the inputs collected • Gain consensus on the points where Data Management must be focused on with priority
Inputs	If available: • Enterprise strategic planning • Strategic initiatives inventory • Regulatory/legal/audit requirements/drivers • Existing Data Strategies
Techniques and Tools	• Collaborative tools for brainstorming and scoring (e.g., Mural, MS365 Whiteboard, etc.) • Brown Paper technique for in-person workshops • Workshop to collect and prioritize business strategic objectives, business questions, data-related behaviors, and data-related pain points
Outputs	• Prioritized business strategic objectives • Prioritized business key questions • Prioritized business drivers/motivations for Data Management • Prioritized data-related undesirable behaviors • Prioritized data-related pain points
Participants	Depending on the scope defined and existing areas: • A representative from each Line of Business • A representative from Corporate Governance • A representative from Legal • A representative from Strategic Planning • A representative from Information Security • A representative from Enterprise Architecture • A representative from IT • Data Governance Lead and team

Step 2. Get Business Insight	
Checkpoint	• Gather all existing documentation for the elements required as input • Prepare your collaborative selected tool or your Brown Paper materials and templates • Prepare an introductory deck clearly indicating the location in the process, and the expectations • Make sure meeting is schedule for the workshop to collect the business insight and confirm attendance • Run the meeting to gather the business insight • Classify information collected during the workshops

7.2.3 Step 3: Build/Update Data Alignment Strategy Canvas

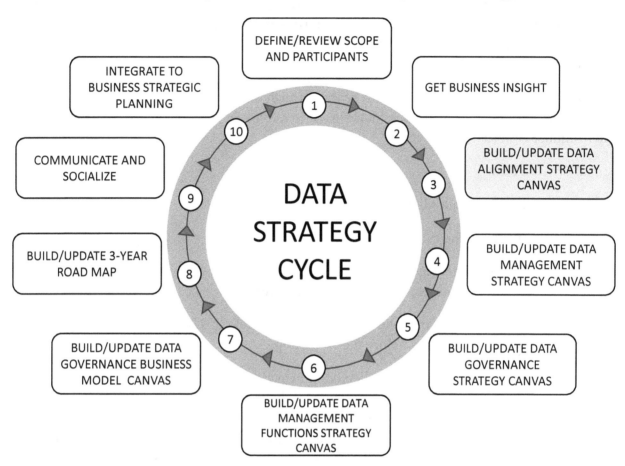

In Step 3, we start defining Data Strategies, beginning with the Data Alignment Strategy (Figure 26). In Step 2, we brought together representatives from all over the organization to prioritize the business strategic objectives and the critical business questions. Step 3 focuses on identifying the data required to respond to these questions, whether it exists or not. This first strategy requires only three of the inputs identified in Step 2:

- Business Strategic Objectives

- Business Questions

- Data-related Pain Points

The Data Alignment Strategy is defined through workshops where all relevant stakeholders participate (Step 2). In preparation for the workshops, the Data Governance lead will populate baseline content (lists) for each Data Alignment Strategy Canvas cell. The participants will add (or perhaps remove) items from these lists. Typically, complete the work in three two-hour sessions. The first two sessions will be to identify the elements for each category and to prioritize them. In the third meeting, present attendees with the canvas filled out with all the input from the previous sessions. At this point, we will make some more adjustments to finalize the canvas. The first time the team goes through the Data Strategy Cycle will be version 1. If the team is engaged in an annual review of the canvas, its starting point will be the existing canvas. The goal of the first meeting will be to identify changes to each cell's content. In the second meeting, the goal will be to review the updated canvas.

Annual reviews are generally easier to work through since the strategy already exists. Still, discussions may require the same number of sessions, depending on the changes in the environment (internal and external).

Step 3 Process Flow

1. Prepare for the Data Alignment Strategy Workshops:

   a. Populate the canvas.

      i. Note: Figure 27 indicates the order to follow when filling out the Data Alignment Strategy Canvas and reading it.

      ii. We defined the content for canvas cells 1, 2, and 3 in Step 2. Populate those cells before the workshop.

      iii. Based on your collected information, prepare a list of items for cells 4-14. At this point, do not worry if the information is incorrect or incomplete. This is just a starting point. If you are reviewing the Data Alignment Strategy as part of the annual review, the starting point is the content approved the previous year.

   b. Prepare your selected collaboration tool with the layout and templates for the workshop and the content of your items lists.

   c. Prepare some slides to open the session. It is appropriate for the first session to set the scene, describing the initiative, participant areas, the mechanics of the sessions, and the goals for the workshops. Don't forget to present the timeline, marking where the session is within it. For subsequent sessions, you can include a summary of the previous session and the goal for the current one.

   d. Confirm sessions are scheduled, and attendees are confirmed. Sessions must not be longer than two hours, so ensure you have a clear agenda with the time assigned to each activity. Designate a timekeeper.

2. Conduct the Workshop Meetings:

   a. At least two sessions are required to capture the content of cells 4-8. Use the first session to work on cells 4, 5, and 6. These steps focus on data domains, data providers, and data consumers.

b. Open the session with your introduction slides to level set the audience's expectations for the session.

c. For each of the cells:

   i. Explain the purpose of the cell and provide some illustrative examples of the content.

   ii. Ask the attendees to write, individually, their ideas of items for the specific cell.

   iii. Give time for all the attendees to read all the ideas from other stakeholders and vote on the five more relevant ones. This will define priority.

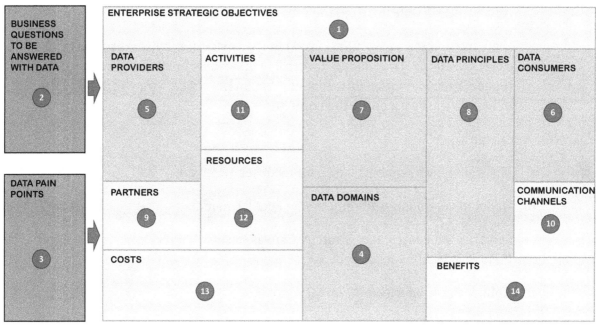

Figure 27 Order to fill out and read Data Alignment Strategy Canvas

3. Fill out the Data Alignment Strategy Canvas:

   a. This is an exercise of synthesis. In cells 4-8, you must fit all the ideas proposed by the stakeholders in the priority order. As noted, cells 4-6 focus on data domains, data producers, and data consumers. Cells 7 and 8 focus on data principles and the value proposition of Data Management. The combination enables you to develop a picture of how to align data to meet business needs. All the materials gathered throughout the journey are the background to sustain the content of this piece of the Data Strategy, so make sure to store them as reference and support.

b. Based on your knowledge of the organization, and the inputs you now have from Steps 1 and 2, you can fill out cells 9-14, which focus on factors required by the Data Management program. (Refer to Chapter 5 to describe what goes in each cell.)

4. Request Feedback:

    a. Conduct the third session with stakeholders to present the complete Data Alignment Strategy Canvas. Get feedback, overall, on cells 9-14, which you did not fill out with them.

    b. Produce your final version of the Data Alignment Strategy Canvas.

    c. Ensure your resulting canvas has valid date and versioning information.

    d. Add a DRAFT watermark to the canvas.

    e. It is time to test your synthesis and clarity capabilities by sending the draft canvas to all the stakeholders for final feedback. Define a deadline for submitting the feedback and make clear that unless you hear back, you will assume the individuals have accepted the content.

5. Get Approval:

    a. Make all the adjustments based on feedback received.

    b. Updated versioning and remove the DRAFT mark.

    c. Send the Data Alignment Strategy Canvas to stakeholders and request approval. Include a deadline for approval.

    d. Collect all the approvals from Stakeholders.

    e. Present results to the sponsor to get approval.

6. Go to Step 9 – Communicate and Socialize

Table 5 Step 3 Summary

Step 3. Build/Update Data Alignment Strategy Canvas	
Objective	• Identify the type of data required to address business needs • Identify data producers and consumers • Identify the Principles on how to manage data • Identify the value proposition of Data Strategies • Identify key activities required to establish a sustainable Data Management Program • Identify high-level costs and benefits of having a Data Management
Purpose	Whether it is the first time this is produced or if it is a subsequent annual review, the purpose of building this Strategy is to: • Align the categories of data (domains) required to address Business Strategic Objectives and Business questions, as well as those related to data pain points • Create consensus on the principles the organization must follow on how to produce and use data • Prioritize the categories of data on which Data Management must be focused • Prioritize the data domains main producers and consumers • Create consensus on the value proposition of Data Strategies and a Data Management Program • Make explicit the key activities and resources needed to materialize the Data Strategies
Inputs	• Prioritized Business Strategic objectives • Classified and prioritized business questions • Prioritized Data Management motivations • Prioritized data-related undesirable behaviors • Prioritized data pain-points
Techniques and Tools	• Workshop to review/update the Data Alignment Strategy • Data Alignment Strategy Canvas template • Collaborative tools for brainstorming and scoring (e.g., Mural, MS365 Whiteboard, etc.) • Brown Paper technique for in-person workshops
Outputs	• Data Alignment Strategy Canvas

Step 3. Build/Update Data Alignment Strategy Canvas	
Participants	<ul><li>Data Governance Lead and team</li><li>A representative from:<ul><li>Each Line of Business</li><li>Corporate Governance</li><li>Legal</li><li>Strategic Planning</li><li>Information Security</li><li>Enterprise Architecture</li><li>IT</li></ul></li></ul>
Checkpoint	<ul><li>Have all the inputs classified and prioritized</li><li>Prepare your collaborative selected tool or your Brown Paper materials and templates</li><li>Prepare an introductory deck clearly indicating the location in the process, and the expectations for this specific step</li><li>Prefill out the Data Alignment Strategy Canvas with the information you have identified so far</li><li>Make sure meeting is schedule for the workshop to review/update the Data Alignment Strategy canvas</li><li>Run the meeting review/update the Data Alignment Strategy</li><li>Get final feedback</li><li>Get approvals</li></ul>

7.2.4 Step 4: Build/Update Data Management Strategy Canvas

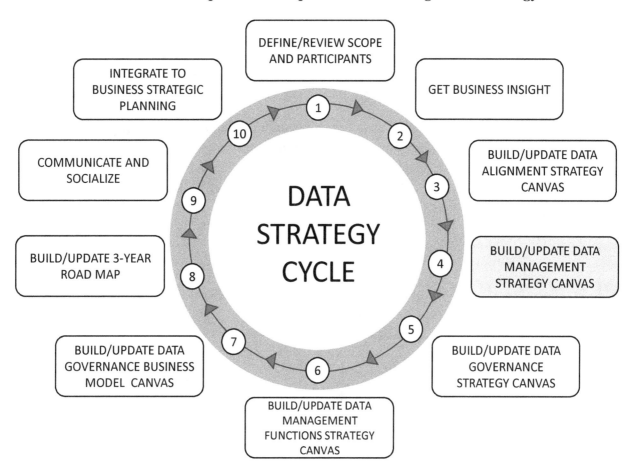

By reaching Step 4, we know the business strategic objectives a good Data Management program can contribute to. We also know the data domains required to support them and the order in which we must address these domains. It is time to identify and prioritize the Data Management Functions to support the program and the business strategy. Prioritizing these functions is fundamental to building out the overall program.

Step 4 is dedicated to producing the Data Management Strategy Canvas based on the drivers or motivations for Data Management (point 2, in Figure 28). It sets expectations for what to achieve for prioritized Data Management functions over a three-year timespan in support of Data Strategy.

Step 4 Process Flow

1. Prepare for the Data Management Strategy workshops:

    a. Based on the inputs from Step 2, the Data Alignment Strategy produced in Step 3, and all the supporting documentation, prepare a list of items for each cell in the canvas shown in Figure 28.

       i. The content for cells 2-5 comes from Step 2.

      ii. For the first workshop session, fill in cell 1 and then draw draft lists for cells 6-14.

     iii. Cells 15-23 will be covered in the second session. If you have content for these, prepare it, but do not populate it until after the first workshop.

b. Prepare your selected collaboration tool with the layout and templates for the workshop and the content of your items lists.

c. Prepare some slides to open the session. It is appropriate for the first session to set the scene, describing the initiative, participant areas, the mechanics of the sessions, and the goals for the workshops. Don't forget to present the timeline, marking where the session is within it. For subsequent sessions, you can include a summary of the previous session and the goal for the current one.

d. Based on the information you have at this time, fill out the Data Management Strategy Canvas (Figure 28).

e. Schedule at least two workshop meetings to have enough time to identify and prioritize the items for cells 1 and 6-23.

f. Verify attendees' confirmation.

2. Conduct the workshop meetings:

a. Use the first session to work on content for cells 1, and 6-14

b. Open the session with your introduction slides to set the audience's expectations.

c. For cell 1:

       i. Explain the purpose of the cell and provide some illustrative examples of the content.

      ii. Ask the attendees to write their ideas of items for the specific cell individually.

     iii. Give time for all the attendees to read all the ideas from other stakeholders and vote on the five more relevant ones.

d. For cells 6-14, use the pre-filled canvas to guide the conversation.

       i. Ask the participants to leave or drop the items listed and suggest new ones.

ii.   Ask the participants to vote for the top three topics; priority will result from this.

3.   Refine the Data Management Strategy Canvas:

a.   Fill cells 2, 3, 4, and 5 with the outcomes from Step 2.

b.   This is an exercise of synthesis. You must fit into cells 1, 6, through 23 of the canvas all the ideas proposed by the stakeholders in the priority order defined in Step 2. (Refer to Chapter 5 for a full description of what goes in each cell.)

4.   Request Feedback:

a.   Ensure your resulting canvas has valid date and versioning information.

b.   Add to the canvas a DRAFT watermark.

c.   Send the filled-out canvas to all the stakeholders that participated in its definition for them to provide feedback. Define a deadline for submitting the feedback and make clear that unless you hear back, you will assume the individuals have accepted the content.

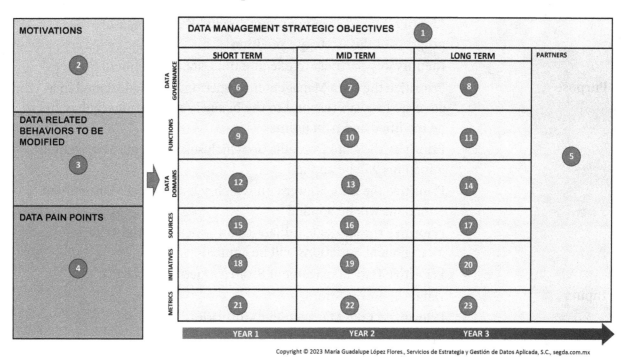

Figure 28 Order to fill out and read The Data Management Strategy Canvas

5.   Get Approval:

a.   Make all the adjustments derived from the feedback received

b. Updated versioning and remove the DRAFT mark

c. Send the Data Management Strategy Canvas for approval from stakeholders participating in the definition. Ensure the deadline is indicated.

d. Collect all the approvals from Stakeholders

e. Present to the sponsor and get approval

6. Go to Step 9 – Communicate and Socialize

Table 6 Step 4 Summary

Step 4. Build/Update Data Management Strategy Canvas	
Objective	• Identify the Data Management Strategic Objectives • Identify the Data Governance Capabilities required to address business needs • Identify the Data Management functions required to address business needs • Identify ongoing strategic initiatives to test Data Management practices • Identify Data Management metrics and KPIs to measure the progress of the strategy execution • Identify key partners to execute the Data Management Strategy
Purpose	• Prioritize the Data Management Functions to be addressed in a governed way to respond to the business motivations, behaviors to be modified and pain points • Prioritize the Data Domains on which selected Data Management Functions will be applied • Prioritize the Data Sources on which selected Data Management Functions will be applied • Prioritize the strategic initiatives on which selected Data Management Functions will be applied • Prioritize Data Management Strategy metrics and KPIs
Inputs	• Data Alignment Strategy • Prioritized Data Management Motivations • Prioritized Data-related Undesirable Behaviors • Prioritized Data Pain Points
Techniques and Tools	• Workshop to review/update the Data Management Strategy • Data Management Strategy Canvas template • Collaborative tools for brainstorming and scoring (e.g., Mural, MS365 Whiteboard, etc.) • Brown Paper technique for in-person workshops

Step 4. Build/Update Data Management Strategy Canvas	
Outputs	• Data Management Strategy Canvas
Participants	• Data Governance Lead and team • A representative from each Line of Business • A representative from Information Security • A representative from Enterprise Architecture • A representative from IT • A representative from the PMO
Checkpoint	• Prepare your collaborative selected tool or your Brown Paper materials and templates • Prepare an introductory deck clearly indicating the location in the process, and the expectations for this specific step • Prefill out the Data Management Strategy Canvas with the information you have identified so far • Make sure meeting is scheduled for the workshop to review/update the Data Management Strategy Canvas • Run the meeting to review/update the Data Management Strategy Canvas • Get final feedback • Get approvals

7.2.5 Step 5: Build/Update Data Governance Strategy Canvas

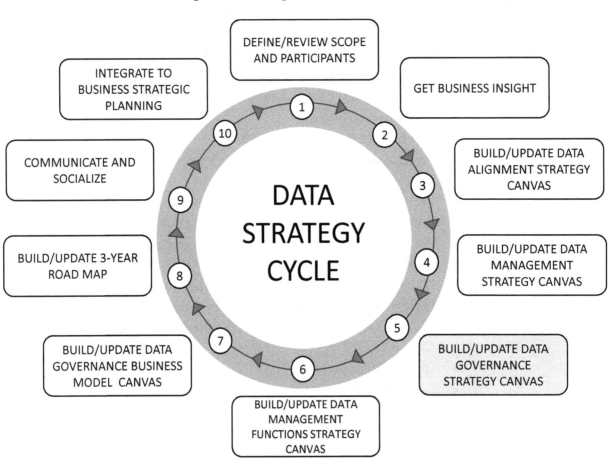

In Step 4, we prioritized the Data Management Functions, starting with Data Governance Capabilities. Step 5 will drill down into the details of Data Governance. All the Data Strategy canvases set expectations for what to achieve over time through the application of Data Management practices. Data Governance is the most visible Data Management function, and it guides the other functions (Data Architecture, Data Quality, Metadata Management, Data integration, etc.). In this step, we will define Data Governance strategic objectives, what capabilities to deploy over time, and who will bring this function to life. One of the most important aspects is to define which objects (business processes, regulatory reports, data repositories, etc.) will be prioritized for governance.

It is highly recommended that, before planning for strategic Data Governance, you have already selected a Data Management Maturity Model focused on capabilities (refer to Chapter 2).

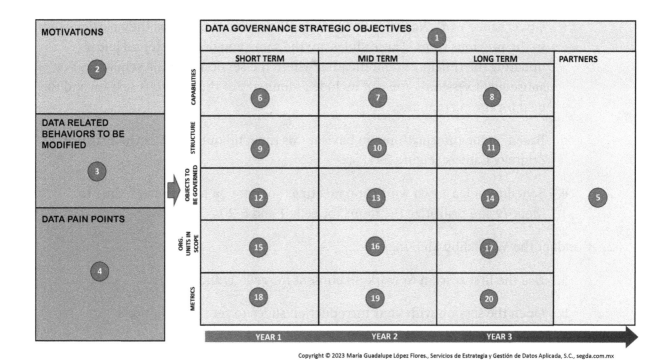

Copyright © 2023 María Guadalupe López Flores., Servicios de Estrategia y Gestión de Datos Aplicada, S.C., segda.com.mx

Figure 29 Order to fill out and read the cells of Data Governance Strategy Canvas

Step 5 Process Flow

1. Prepare for the Data Governance Strategy Workshops:

   a. Based on the inputs produced in Step 2, the Data Alignment Strategy produced in Step 3, the Data Management Strategy produced in Step 4, and all the supporting documentation, prepare a list of items for each cell in the canvas shown in Figure 29.

      i. From Step 2, you get the content for cells 2,3, 4, and 5.

      ii. You may want to refine cell 5 to identify the partners supporting Data Governance (e.g., the Project Management Office, Internal Communication, Internal Audit, Compliance, etc.).

      iii. For the first workshop session, prepare to start with cell 1 and cover cells 6-11. We will cover cells 12-20 in the second session.

   b. Prepare your selected collaboration tool with the layout and templates for the workshop and the content from your items lists.

   c. Prepare some slides to open the session. It is appropriate for the first session to set the scene, describing the initiative, participant areas, the mechanics of the sessions, and the goals of the workshops. This will be useful for documenting all the exercises for future reference. The stakeholders participating in the Data

Governance workshop should be aware of all the initiatives as they participated in the previous steps. These slides are the same you used in steps 3 and 4, updating the timeline and indicating where the session is in the sequence. For subsequent sessions, you can include a summary of the previous session and the goal for the current one.

    d. Based on the information you have at this time, fill out the Data Governance Strategy Canvas (Figure 29).

    e. Schedule at least two workshop meetings so that you have enough time to identify and prioritize the items for cells 1 and 6-20.

2.   Conduct the Workshop Meetings:

    a. Use the first session to work on content for cells 1, and 6 to 11

    b. Open the session with your introduction slides to set the audience's expectations.

    c. For cell 1:

        i. Explain the purpose of the cell and provide some illustrative examples of the content.

        ii. Ask the attendees to write their ideas of items for the specific cell individually.

        iii. Give time for all the attendees to read all the ideas from other stakeholders and vote on the five more relevant ones.

    d. For cells 6 to 11, use the pre-filled canvas to guide the conversation.

        i. Ask the participants to retain or remove the items listed and suggest new ones.

        ii. Ask the participants to vote for the top three topics.

3.   Refine the Data Governance Strategy Canvas:

    a. Fill cells 2, 3, 4, and 5 with the outcomes from Step 2.

    b. This is an exercise of synthesis. You must fit into cells 1 and 6, through 23 of the canvas, all the ideas proposed by the stakeholders in the order of priority they suggested. (Refer to Chapter 5 to describe what goes in each cell.)

4.   Request Feedback

    a. Ensure your resulting canvas has proper date and versioning information.

    b. Add to the canvas a DRAFT watermark.

    c. It is time to test your synthesis and clarity capabilities by sending the filled-out canvas to all the stakeholders that participated in its definition for them to provide feedback. Define a deadline for submitting the feedback and make clear that unless you hear back, you will assume the individuals have accepted the content.

5. Get Approval

    a. Make all the adjustments derived from the feedback received

    b. Updated versioning and remove the DRAFT mark

    c. Send the Data Governance Strategy Canvas for approval from stakeholders participating in the definition. Ensure the deadline is indicated.

    d. Collect all the approvals from stakeholders

    e. Present to the sponsor and get approval

6. Go to Step 9 – Communicate and Socialize

Table 7 Step 5 Summary

Step 5. Define/Update Data Governance Strategy Canvas	
Objective	• Identify the Data Governance Strategic Objectives • Confirm and complement the Data Governance Capabilities identified in the Data Management Strategy required to address business needs, modify data-related behaviors, or remediate data-related pain points • Identify the organizational structure required for running the Data Governance practice • Identify the objects (processes, reports, data repositories, data sources, data domains, etc.) to be Governed • Identify the business units to adopt the Data Governance practice • Identify Data Management metrics and KPIs to measure the progress of the strategy execution • Identify key partners to execute the Data Governance Strategy

Step 5. Define/Update Data Governance Strategy Canvas	
Purpose	• Prioritize the Data Governance capabilities to be established over the time in the organization • Prioritize the Data Governance roles and governance bodies to be assigned/established over the time and the areas in the organization where they will be acting • Prioritize the data-related objects that will be governed within the organization • Prioritize the organizational units where the Data Governance practice will be implemented • Prioritize Data Governance Strategy metrics and KPIs
Inputs	• Data Alignment Strategy • Data Management Strategy • Prioritized Data Management motivations • Prioritized data-related undesired behaviors • Prioritized data pain-points
Techniques and Tools	• Workshop to review/update the Data Governance Strategy • Data Governance Strategy Canvas template • Collaborative tools for brainstorming and scoring (e.g., Mural, MS365 Whiteboard, etc.) • Brown paper technique for in-person workshops
Outputs	• Data Governance Strategy Canvas
Participants	• Data Governance Lead and team • A representative of the Data Management functions identified as a priority (if they exist)
Checkpoint	• Prepare your collaborative selected tool or your Brown Paper materials and templates • Prepare an introductory deck clearly indicating the location in the process, and the expectations for this specific step • Prefill out the Data Governance Strategy Canvas with the information you have identified so far • Schedule meeting for the workshop to review/update the Data Governance Strategy Canvas • Run the meeting to review/update the Data Management Strategy • Get final feedback • Get approvals

7.2.6 Step 6: Build/Update Specific Data Management Function Strategy Canvas

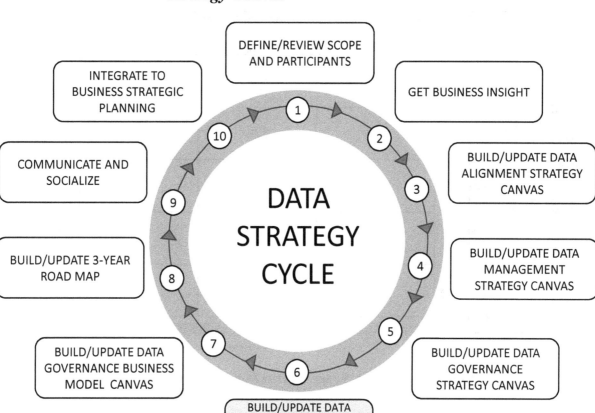

Data Management Functions were prioritized as part of producing the Data Management Strategy Canvas. Some of these functions may already be in place. For example, some level of Data Storage and Operations, as well as Data Integration, typically exist. The existence of these functions does not mean that they are mature, adequately governed, or strategically aligned. Different functions will be at different levels of maturity. The strategy will therefore associate them with different kinds of goals. For example, if Metadata Management does not exist, then the short-term goal will be to get initial capabilities established. If Data Storage already exists, the short-term goals will include developing policies and rules to ensure processes are properly governed. As described through comparison to the three-legged stool in Chapter 5, it is best to address no more than three Data Management Functions at a time, with Data Governance always being one of those three.

Data Governance Strategy was discussed in Step 5. Next, define a strategy for each other priority Data Management Functions. The Specific Data Management Function Strategy Canvas (Figure 30), is very similar to the Data Governance Strategy Canvas (Figure 29). You can see that once you produce the Data Management Strategy Canvas, the rest will come more easily. They are all tied together by the same connecting threads: the business motivations, the data-related pain points, and the data behaviors to modify. These influence lists develop in cells 6-20.

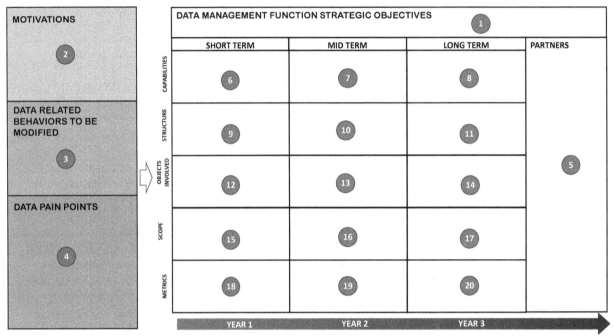

Figure 30 Order to fill out and read The Specific Data Management Function Strategy Canvas

Step 6 Process Flow

1. Prepare for the Specific Data Management Function Strategy Workshops:

    a. Based on the inputs from Step 2, the Data Alignment Strategy produced in Step 3, the Data Management Strategy produced in Step 4, the Data Governance Strategy defined in Step 5, and all the supporting documentation, prepare a list of items for each cell in the canvas shown in Figure 30.

        i. From Step 2, you get the content for cells 2-5. In this case, again, you may need to refine cell 5 with specific Partners.

        ii. For the first workshop session, you must prepare to start with cell 1 and then go from 6-11.

        iii. Cells 12-20 will be covered in the second session.

    b. Prepare your selected collaboration tool with the layout for the workshop and the content of your items lists.

    c. Prepare slides to open the session. It is appropriate for the first session to set the scenario, describing the initiative, participant areas, the mechanics of the sessions, and the goal to reach after the workshops. Most stakeholders participating in this step have <u>not</u> participated in previous ones, so the context will be necessary and welcome. Don't forget to present the timeline, marking where the session is within it. For subsequent sessions, you can include a summary of the previous session and the goal for the current one.

    d. Based on the information you have at this time, fill out the Specific Data Management Function Strategy Canvas (Figure 30).

    e. Schedule at least two workshop meetings to have enough time to identify and prioritize the items for cells 1 and 6-20

2. Conduct the Workshop Meetings:

    a. Use the first session to work on content for cells 1, and 6 to 11

    b. Open the session with your introduction slides to set the audience's expectations.

    c. For cell 1:

        i. Explain the purpose of the cell and provide some illustrative examples of the content.

        ii. Ask the attendees to write their ideas of items for the specific cell individually.

        iii. Give time for all the attendees to read all the ideas from other stakeholders and vote on the five more relevant ones.

    d. For cells 6-11, use the pre-filled canvas to guide the conversation.

        i. Ask the participants to leave or drop the items listed and suggest new ones.

        ii. Ask the participants to vote for the top three topics.

3. Refine the Specific Data Management Function Strategy Canvas:

    a. Fill cells 2-5 with the outcomes from Step 2. Cell 5 may change based on the additional input you got from the first session of this step.

    b. You must fit into cells 1 and 6, through 23 of the canvas, all the ideas proposed by the stakeholders in the order of priority they suggested. (Refer to Chapter 5 for the description of what goes in each cell.)

4. Request Feedback:

a. Ensure your resulting canvas has valid date and versioning information.

b. Add to the canvas a DRAFT watermark.

c. It is time to test your synthesis and clarity capabilities by sending the filled-out canvas to all the stakeholders that participated in its definition for them to provide feedback. Define a deadline for submitting the feedback and make clear that unless you hear back, you will assume the individuals have accepted the content.

5. Get Approval:

a. Make all the adjustments derived from the feedback received

b. Updated versioning and remove the DRAFT mark

c. Send the Specific Data Management Function Canvas for approval from stakeholders participating in the definition. Ensure the deadline is indicated.

d. Collect all the approvals from Stakeholders

e. Present to sponsor and get approval

6. Go to Step 9 – Communicate and Socialize

Table 8 Step 6 Summary

Step 6. Build/Update Specific Data Management Function Strategy	
Objective	<ul><li>Identify the Specific Data Management Function Strategic Objectives</li><li>Identify the Specific Data Management Function's capabilities required to address business needs, modify data-related behaviors, or remediate data-related pain points</li><li>Identify the organizational structure required for running the Specific Data Management Function practice</li><li>Identify the objects (processes, reports, data repositories, data sources, data domains, etc.) on which the Specific Data Management Function will be applied</li><li>Identify the scope or extent to which the Specific Data Management Function will be applied</li><li>Identify Specific Data Management Function metrics and KPIs to measure the progress of the strategy execution</li><li>Identify key partners for the Specific Data Management Function Strategy</li></ul>

Step 6. Build/Update Specific Data Management Function Strategy	
Purpose	• Prioritize the Specific Data Management Function capabilities to be established over the time in the organization • Prioritize the Specific Data Management Function roles and governance bodies to be assigned/established over the time and the areas in the organization where they will be acting • Prioritize the data-related objects to which this Specific Data Management Function will be applied • Prioritize the organizational units where the Specific Data Management Function will be deployed • Prioritize Specific Data Management Function Strategy metrics and KPIs
Inputs	• Data Alignment Strategy • Data Management Strategy • Data Governance Strategy • Data Governance Business Model • Prioritized Data Management motivations • Prioritized data-related undesired behaviors • Prioritized data pain-points
Techniques and Tools	• Workshop to review/update the Specific Data Management Roadmap • Specific Data Management Function Canvas template • Collaborative tools for brainstorming and scoring (e.g., Mural, MS365 Whiteboard, etc.) • Brown paper technique for in-person workshops
Outputs	• Specific Data Management Function Canvas
Participants	• Data Governance Lead and Team • Specific Data Management Function Team
Checkpoint	• Prepare your collaborative selected tool or your Brown paper materials and templates • Prepare an introductory deck clearly indicating the location in the process, and the expectations for this specific step • Prefill out the Specific Data Management Function Canvas with the information you have identified so far • Make sure meeting is scheduled for the workshop to review/update the Specific Data Management Function Canvas • Run the meeting to review/update the Specific Data Management Function Canvas

7.2.7 Step 7: Build/Update Data Governance Business Model Canvas

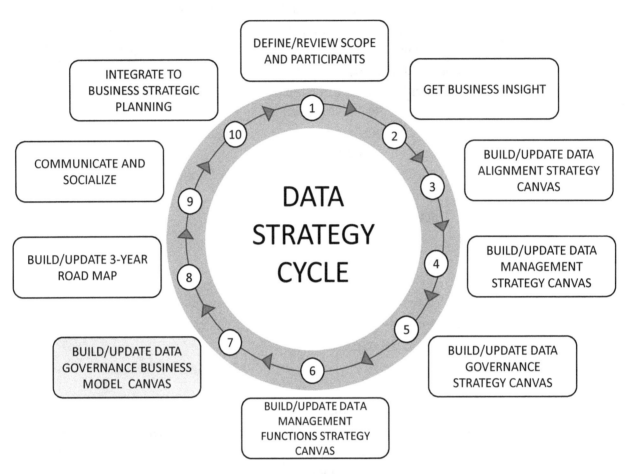

In Chapter 5, we discussed the power behind Alexander Osterwalder's Business Model Canvas and why it became the prime source of inspiration for the Data Strategy Canvases. You can apply it not only to large and small organizations but also to all types of individual functions within an organization. For any function you want to name, there is always a customer being served, a value proposition for that customer, and activities to do to fulfill that proposition. This is why you can model all the Data Management Functions using this canvas. Data Governance is the central Data Management Function. Having an approach to it is required to formalize the other Data Management Functions, so we use it to describe this cycle step. All the other Data Management Functions will also have their own Business Model Canvas. Documenting these Business Models contributes significantly to building teams, as they set what to do, for whom, who will help on the road, how much it will cost, and what the benefits will be.

Figure 31 shows the generic Business Model Canvas with the inputs identified and prioritized in Step 2.

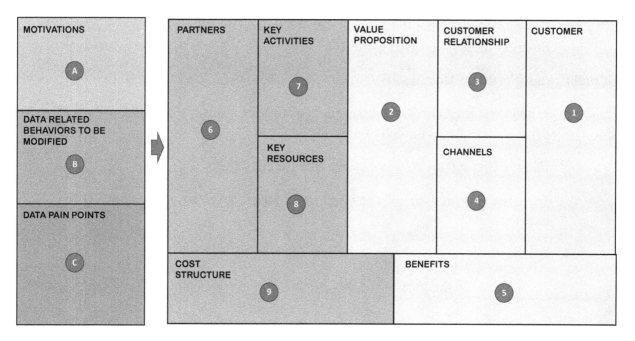

Figure 31 Data Governance Business Model

Step 7 Process Flow

1. Prepare for the Data Governance Business Model Workshops:

    a. Based on the inputs from Step 2, the Data Alignment Strategy produced in Step 3, the Data Management Strategy produced in Step 4, the Data Governance Strategy produced in Step 5, and all the supporting documentation, prepare a list of items for each cell in the canvas shown in Figure 31.

        i. From Step 2, you get the content for cells A, B, and C.

        ii. For the first workshop session, you must be prepared to start with cell 1 and then go from 1 to 5.

        iii. Cells 6-9 might require another session.

    b. Prepare your selected collaboration tool with the layout for the workshop and the content of your items lists.

    c. Prepare slides to open the session. Even though the stakeholders participating have been present at the previous steps, it is helpful to have a presentation updated for this session and to be left as documentation for future reference. Don't forget to present the timeline, marking where the session is within it. For subsequent sessions, you can include a summary of the previous session and the goal for the current one.

    d. Based on the information you have at this time, fill out the Data Governance Business Model Canvas (Figure 31).

2. Conduct the Workshop Meetings:

    a. Schedule at least two workshop meetings to have enough time to identify and prioritize the items for cells 1 and 6-9

    b. Use the first session to work on content for cells 1-5

    c. Open the session with your introduction slides to level set the audience's expectations.

    d. For cell 1:

        i. Explain the purpose of the cell and provide some illustrative examples of the content.

        ii. Ask the attendees to write their ideas of items for the specific cell individually.

        iii. Give time for all the attendees to read all the ideas from other stakeholders and vote on the five more relevant ones.

    e. For cells 6 to 11, use the pre-filled canvas to guide the conversation.

        i. Ask the participants to leave or drop the items listed and suggest new ones.

        ii. Ask the participants to vote for the top three topics.

3. Refine the Data Governance Strategy Canvas:

    a. Fill cells 2, 3, 4, and 5 with the outcomes from Step 2.

    b. This is an exercise of synthesis. You must fit into cells 1, and 6, through 23 of the canvas, all the ideas proposed by the stakeholders in the order of priority they suggested. (Refer to Chapter 5 for the description of what goes in each cell.)

4. Request Feedback:

    a. Ensure your resulting canvas has proper date and versioning information.

    b. Add to the canvas a DRAFT watermark.

    c. It is time to test your synthesis and clarity capabilities by sending the filled-out canvas to all the stakeholders that participated in its definition for them to provide feedback. Define a deadline for submitting the feedback and make clear that unless you hear back, you will assume the individuals have accepted the content.

5.Get Approval

    a. Make all the adjustments derived from the feedback received

    b. Updated versioning and remove the DRAFT mark

    c. Send the Data Alignment Strategy Canvas for approval from stakeholders participating in the definition. Ensure the deadline is indicated.

    d. Collect all the approvals from Stakeholders

    e. Present to the sponsor and get approval

6.Go to Step 9 – Communicate and Socialize

Table 9 Step 7 Summary

Step 7. Build/Update Data Governance Business Model Canvas	
Objective	<ul><li>Identify Data Governance Customers</li><li>Identify Data Governance Value Proposition</li><li>Identify Data Governance Services through which provide the Value Proposition</li><li>Identify Data Governance team communication channels with its customers</li><li>Identify how to maintain relationships to retain interest and recognition from customers</li><li>Identify key activities required to deliver on the Value Proposition</li><li>Identify the key resources required to deliver on the Value Proposition</li><li>Identify the key partners to support the Data Governance team in its endeavor to deploy the Data Governance practice</li><li>Make explicit at a high level, the cost of deploying and sustaining the Data Governance practice</li><li>Make explicit at a high level, the benefits of having a Data Governance practice</li></ul>
Purpose	<ul><li>Set clear expectations across all the organization on what the Data Governance team will be doing and for which internal customers.</li></ul>
Inputs	<ul><li>Data Alignment Strategy</li><li>Data Management Strategy</li><li>Prioritized Data Management motivations</li><li>Prioritized data-related undesireable behaviors</li><li>Prioritized data pain-points</li></ul>

Step 7. Build/Update Data Governance Business Model Canvas	
Techniques and Tools	• Workshop to review/update the Data Governance Business Model • Business Model Canvas template • Collaborative tools for brainstorming and scoring (e.g., Mural, MS365 Whiteboard, etc.) • Brown paper technique for in-person workshops
Outputs	• Data Governance Business Model Canvas
Participants	• Data Governance Lead and team
Checkpoint	• Prepare your collaborative selected tool or your Brown paper materials and templates • Prepare an introductory deck clearly indicating the location in the process, and the expectations for this specific step • Prefill out the Data Governance Business Model Canvas with the information you have identified so far • Make sure meeting is scheduled for the workshop to review/update the Data Governance Business Model Canvas • Run the meeting to review/update the Data Governance Business Model

7.2.8 Step 8: Build/Update 3-Year Roadmap

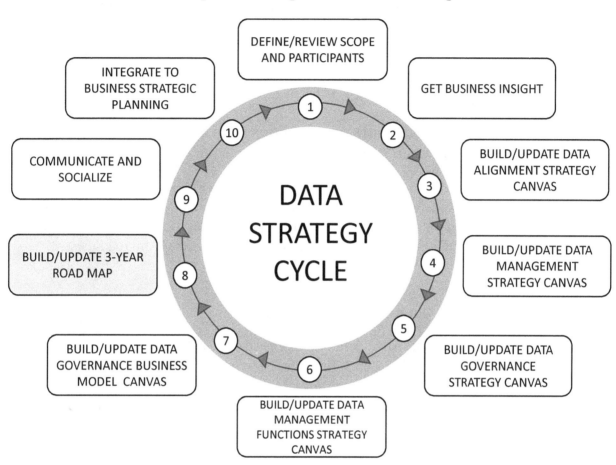

Developing the Data Management Strategy Canvases (Data Management Strategy, Data Governance Strategy, and Specific Data Management Function Strategy) is essential to managing expectations about what to achieve over time through the Data Management program. But the best way to clearly show what to expect at different points in time is through roadmaps. Since the Data Governance team orchestrates the definition of the other Data Management functions, the first roadmap to develop is the Data Governance Roadmap (Figures 32, 33, and 34). Once this roadmap and the Data Management Function Strategies are defined, a roadmap can be produced for each function.

The milestones in the roadmap come directly from the Data Management Strategy and the Data Governance Strategy, surrounded by milestones marked in green representing the operation of Data Governance. This is important for setting and managing expectations. It must be clear that we are not spending one or two years just establishing Data Governance capabilities. In parallel, we are starting to operate governance, following priorities established in the Data Management and Data Governance Strategies.

A formal capabilities-based Data Management Maturity model is crucial for this. The combination of clearly defined capabilities and the maturity level targets anchors milestones in the roadmaps. This way, we can represent annual goals and progress prioritized capabilities.

The Year 1 Roadmap starts with the maturity levels determined by the baseline maturity assessment. The end of this first year shows the maturity level the organization expects to reach, based on projected milestones.

The Year 2 Roadmap starts with the maturity level measured at the end of the Year 1 Roadmap. It ends with the estimated maturity level based on projected milestones. This maturity level becomes the starting point for Year 3 Roadmap.

After the first year of Data Governance operations, perform the data management maturity assessment (Ideally based on evidence rather than just perception to remove any subjectivity) to determine the actual maturity reached. Use this information to adjust the roadmap.

Step 8 Process Flow

1. Prepare for the Data Governance Roadmap Workshops:

    a. Based on the Data Alignment Strategy produced in Step 3, the Data Management Strategy produced in Step 4, the Data Governance Strategy produced in Step 5, and the Data Governance capabilities indicated by the Data Management Maturity model you have selected, prepare a draft of the three-year roadmap. Input also includes the current maturity level based on the most recent assessment.

    b. Start by setting the Data Governance capabilities milestones.

    c. From the Data Management Strategy, determine milestones related to the priorities segregated along the short, mid, and long term, and set them along the roadmap.

    d. Do the same for the Data Governance Strategy; determine milestones related to the priorities segregated along the short, mid, and long term, and set them along the roadmap.

    e. Based on the inputs provided to create the Data Management and the Data Governance Strategies, identify milestones indicating that Data Governance is operating (Business Glossary published, Data Governance Committee first meeting, Data Source inquiry service established, first set of Policies approved, etc.)

2. Conduct the Workshop Meetings:

    a. Schedule at least two workshop meetings to have enough time to complete and refine the Data Governance Roadmap.

    b. Use the first session to complement the list of milestones along the Data Governance Roadmap and to create awareness of the work required. Be realistic. Many teams plan for too many milestones in the first year. Doing so and not meeting them can be discouraging. Try not to overcommit.

    c. Use the second session to refine the roadmap, ensuring all necessary milestones are documented and achievable as distributed over the three years. This distribution must align with the priority defined in the Data Management and Data Governance Strategies while also accounting for dependencies.

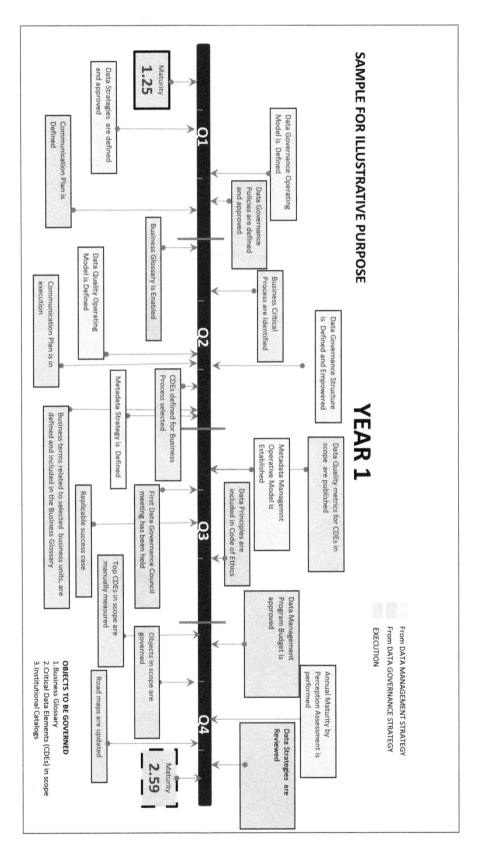

Figure 32 Data Governance Roadmap for year 1

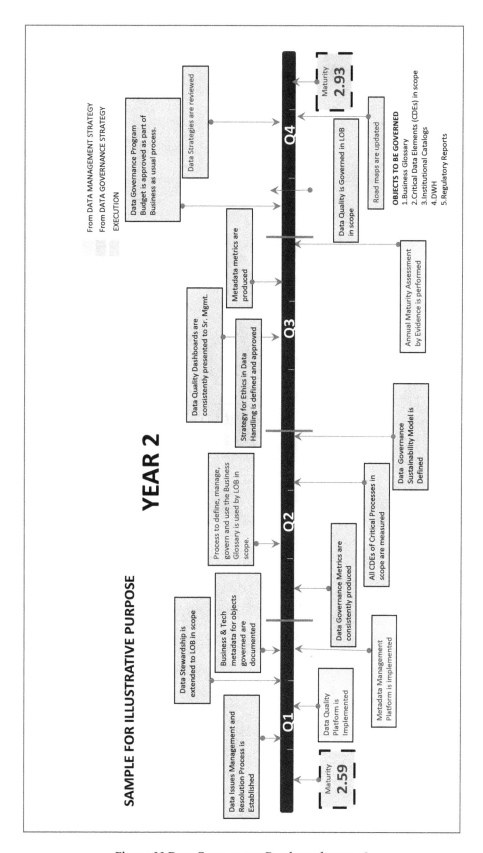

Figure 33 Data Governance Roadmap for year 2

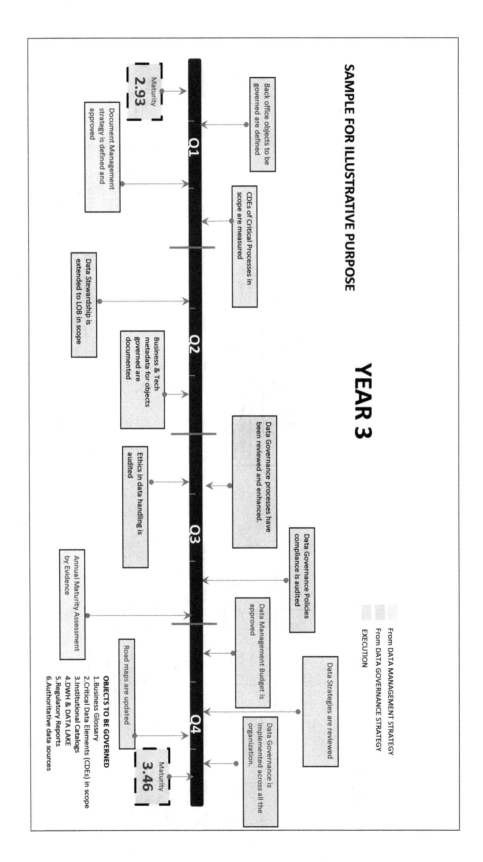

Figure 34 Data Governance Roadmap for year 3

3. Get Approval:

    a. Make all the adjustments derived from the feedback received

    b. Updated versioning and remove the DRAFT mark

    c. Send the Data Governance Roadmap for approval from the sponsor

4. Go to Step 9 – Communicate and Socialize

Table 10 Step 8 Summary

Step 8. Build/Update 3-Year Roadmap	
Objective	• Identify milestones to be accomplished in the next three years, based on the Data Management and Data Governance Strategies • Set the expected Data Management maturity level for each year, based on milestones for capabilities to be established
Purpose	• Set clear expectations across all the organization on what is going to be accomplished and when as part of the execution of Data Management and Data Governance Strategies
Inputs	• Data Alignment Strategy • Data Management Strategy • Data Governance Strategy • Data Governance Business Model • Prioritized Data Management motivations • Prioritized data-related undesired behaviors • Prioritized data pain-points
Techniques and Tools	• Workshop to review/update the Data Management Roadmap • Workshop to review/update the Data Governance Roadmap • Data Management Roadmap template • Data Governance Roadmap template • Collaborative tools for brainstorming and scoring (e.g., Mural, MS365 Whiteboard, etc.) • Brown paper technique for in-person workshops • Mapping technique to link to Operational Plan
Outputs	• Data Management three-year roadmap • Data Governance three-year roadmap

Step 8. Build/Update 3-Year Roadmap	
Participants	For the Data Management Roadmap: • Data Management Lead • Data Governance Lead and Team • Data Management functions prioritized For Data Governance Roadmap: • Data Governance Lead and Team
Checkpoint	• Prepare your collaborative selected tool or your Brown paper materials and templates • Prepare an introductory deck clearly indicating the location in the process, and the expectations for this specific step • Draft the Data Management Roadmap to start discussion • Schedule meetings for the workshop to review/update the Data Management and the Data Governance Roadmaps • Run the meeting to review/update the Data Management and the Data Governance Roadmaps

7.2.9 Step 9: Communicate and Socialize

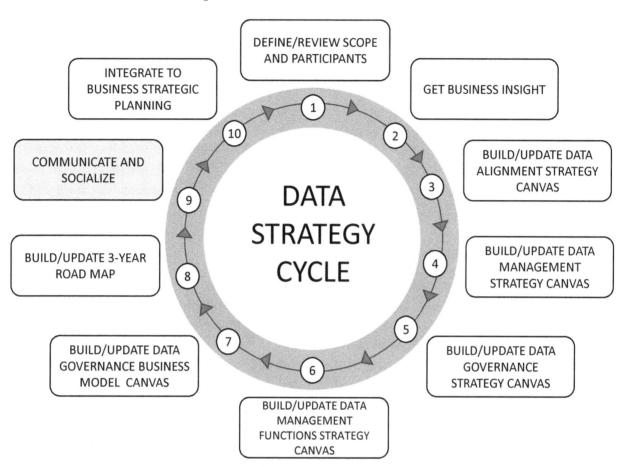

A fundamental piece of this puzzle is communication. We have discussed the benefits of using canvases to facilitate communication. Canvases would be worthless if we produced them and kept them in a drawer. The Data Strategy initiative is a continuous process that must be widely communicated across the organization. For it to be successful, it must have a clear Communication Strategy. This strategy starts with objectives. Identify the different audiences who need to keep informed about what is happening in Data Management. Account for the range of communications media through which to reach them. Not only electronic (e.g., intranet, email) but also the different forums where you can present this topic or internal events where you can communicate Data Strategy. If a corporate or institutional communication area exists, engage with them on the effort.

Communication is barely considered when implementing Data Governance and even less when discussing Data Management. But it is essential to success. Failure to plan communications means that many stakeholders do not understand what it means to govern data, what the Data Management Functions do and oversee, what services they offer, and what to expect from the services.

In the Communicate and Socialize step, you define your marketing for Data Strategy. For this, you must consider the following:

- Target audiences

- Types of messages to be communicated

- The availability and effectiveness of various communications media

- Communications Forums (e.g., steering or standing committees)

- Organizational Culture

- Communication policies

- Communication campaigns plans

Remember that communication is all about people – you want to deliver your messages to stakeholders. Identifying the communication channels available is important, but more important is understanding how effective they are. For example, if an internal website exists, but employees rarely visit it, it is not an effective channel. If you want to use it, give people a reason to visit it. Email is an easy and common communication channel. But most people receive many emails that they do not read. By using email, you risk having your messages fade without being seen. If the number of messages is high, those will be ignored. If there's already a website for Data Management or Data Governance purposes, that will be an excellent place to post information about the Data Strategy initiative, its status, and the different canvases produced. If there's no site yet, you may want to start one as part of this initiative. In any case, you must make people aware of its existence and promote its use.

Step 9 Process Flow

1. Define the Communication Strategy:

    a. The strategic objectives you want to achieve

    b. The audiences you want to reach

    c. The communication channels available

    d. The partners to help you communicate

    e. The types of messages you want to communicate

        i. Awareness: Internal infographics of impacts derived from lack of Data Management

        ii. Informative: Definition of Data Strategy elements

      iii. Initiative progress: Updates on Data Strategies execution progress

2. Engage Institutional Communication Team:

    a. The most effective communication channels for executing the communication strategy.

    b. The level of participation of the institutional communication team

    c. The level of approval required for communication messages

    d. The best communication campaigns

    e. The policies to be followed if messages are not communicated from the institutional team

    f. The operational interaction your team can have with the institutional team

3. Explore New Ideas:

    a. Lunch and learn meetings (in person or virtual)

    b. Internal podcast (invite stakeholders with success stories)

    c. Data Strategy Nuggets (short informative messages with attractive designs to capture the attention)

4. Engage Data Strategy sponsor in Communication:

    a. Have the sponsor record strong messages around Data Strategy

    b. Have the sponsor establish standing participation in steering committees to present progress in Data Strategies

5. Define a Content Grid:

    a. Type of message

    b. Objective of message

    c. Copy (actual message as it is going to be transmitted)

    d. Call to action

    e. The date on which the message will be communicated

6. Create a Communication Plan

    a. Consider all different communication channels and creative alternatives

b. Consider any ongoing or planned institutional communication campaigns

c. Consider approvals time response

7. Execute the Communication Plan

Table 11 Step 9 Summary

Step 9. Communicate and Socialize	
Objective	• Establish a Communications Strategy • Engage the enterprise's internal communication team • Ensure all stakeholders see the results of their contributions to the Data Strategies • Make sure people across the organization know about the Data Strategies • Ensure the Data Strategies canvases are easy to find and access
Purpose	• Ensure the Data Strategy is open to all the organization • Set expectations across the organization about what will be achieved by Data Management and Data Governance programs
Inputs	• Data Alignment Strategy • Data Management Strategy • Data Governance Strategy • Data Governance Business Model • Specific Data Management Strategy
Techniques and Tools	• Content Grid • Executive debrief • Communication strategy template
Outputs	• Data Management Communication Strategy • Data Strategies content Grid • Communication content
Participants	• Institutional Communication • Data Governance Lead and team
Checkpoint	• Define your Communication Strategy • Engage Internal Communication team • Collect sound information of data issues and their impact • Prepare your Content Matrix • Define a Communication Plan • Get approval • Execute the plan

7.2.10 Step 10: Integrate into existing Business Strategic Planning

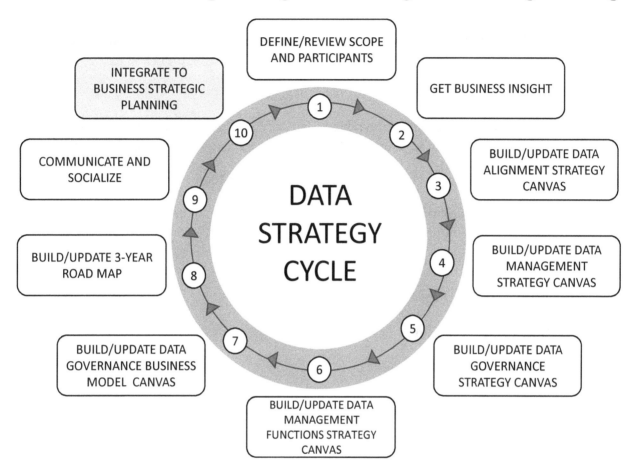

A critical characteristic of a mature Data Management Program is sustainability. This implies having an annual budget to support Data Management practices. The annual budget requirements must be well understood within a continuous and evolving deployment of capabilities. The last thing we want is to explain Data Management from scratch for every project within the program. Instead, Step 10 seeks to integrate Data Management goals and initiatives into strategic planning so that these are always part of the planning cycle.

The other fundamental rationale for this step is that we must align Data Strategy with the enterprise strategy. As part of annual strategic planning, key stakeholders analyze the business environment and set strategic direction for the organization. Data must be accounted for as part of this process, and the sponsor of Data Management must have a seat at this table. To bring this about requires engaging leaders in strategic planning and finance through a strong business case.

Step 10 Process Flow

1. Create a Business Case:

    a. Quantify the impact of the top data-related pain points

b. Quantify the cost of opportunity for not being able to respond to the top-priority business questions

c. Quantify the impact of not having a Data Strategy (based on past cases of technological platforms bought without fully utilizing them)

d. Quantify the cost of not finding information

e. Quantify the benefits of having a Data Strategy, not only in terms of cost avoidance but also in terms of the business value of having accurate insights

2. Prepare a Charter for each Data Management Initiative Identified for the Short Term

3. Prepare an Annual Budget to Cover Data Governance Deployment and Support, and Each of the Charters Identified

4. Prepare an Executive Summary Supported on:

a. Data Strategy Charter

b. Organizational units participating

c. Data Governance Roadmap

d. Link to Data Strategy Canvases

e. Annual Budget

5. Engage the Strategic Planning Team:

a. Have the Data Strategy sponsor introduce the Data Strategy initiative

b. Agree on how, when, and to whom the progress of the Data Strategy will be reported

c. Collect feedback

d. Define a high-level process on how the Data Strategy process will be embedded in the enterprise planning process

e. Get feedback on the proposed process

f. Get approval

g. Go to Step 9 to communicate the final process

Table 12 Step 10 Summary

Step 10. Integrate into existing Business Strategic Planning	
Objective	• Embed Data Strategy into the Enterprise Strategic Planning • Create awareness of data assets to be treated as any other assets • Create awareness of Data Management being a Program that requires ongoing funding
Purpose	• Engagement with Corporate Planning • Engagement with Finance
Inputs	• Data Alignment Strategy • Data Management Strategy • Data Governance Strategy
Techniques and Tools	• Executive debrief
Outputs	• Timeline of annual Data Strategies review
Participants	• Data Strategy Sponsor • Data Governance Lead and team • Corporate Planning • Finance
Checkpoint	• Document your business case • Prepare an executive presentation of the Data Strategy process and the approved Data Strategies • Engage the Enterprise Strategic Planning team • Establish agreement on how to embed Data Strategy into Enterprise Strategic Planning • Engage the Finance team • Establish agreement on how to manage an annual budget for Data Management, based on Data Strategies

7.3.   A Few Words on Tools

All the canvases we have shown rely on PowerPoint templates, providing an easy way to start. As you may have already thought, there are better, more dynamic, and more agile ways to represent canvases. Most Enterprise Architecture tools allow you to create customized canvases and link them to other enterprise artifacts (enterprise strategy, business processes, roles, governing bodies, application architectures, technology architectures, etc.). These tools allow you to capture the content of the canvases and document how, when, and by whom they were created. These can also show traceability online, so changes are also reflected in linked objects when a certain object changes. There are also open-source options if you do not have an

Enterprise Architecture Tool. Once you create your Data Strategy Canvases, such tools allow you to export each canvas as an image to facilitate organizational communication.

You may also explore options for collaboration tools that simplify the capture and use of information in the workshops.

7.4.   Connecting All the Dots

All the elements in the three components of The Data Strategy PAC Method are connected. You should be able to trace between them at any time. For example, when you produce an operational plan for the Data Strategies, map each activity to a milestone in the roadmaps. The milestones in the roadmaps come from each Data Strategy Canvas. The content of each Data Strategy Canvas responds to the inputs defined in the second step of the Data Strategy Cycle: Business questions, motivations, behaviors to be changed, and data-related pain points. As you progress through the Data Strategy Cycle, you will notice this interconnection and how everything makes sense. As you communicate with stakeholders, draw attention to these connections to help them understand the goals and details required to achieve them.

Maintaining an effective Data Strategy is a continuous process. The work does not end once you have produced the Data Strategy Canvases. The hard work of execution starts at that point. That work entails overseeing that the strategies guide data-related activities and enable the organization to get more value from its data.

7.5.   Key Concepts

The Data Strategy Cycle is a set of ten steps that must be taken at least annually, ending up on including the Data Strategies review in the organization's annual strategic planning. This significantly contributes to managing data and information as strategic assets.

7.6.   Things to Keep in Mind

1.   The first success factor is having key stakeholders representing the various organizational units participating in the definition of the Data Alignment Strategy, as their input and prioritization will drive the rest of the Data Strategies.

2.   The second success factor is effective preparation of each workshop meeting and time management during the sessions.

3. The third and not less important success factor is maintaining effective communication with all the stakeholders participating in this journey so they are aware of how their contribution turns into Data Strategies and how they are executed over time.

 ## 7.7. Interview on Data Strategy

EXPERT INTERVIEWED: **Danette McGilvray**[45]

Danette McGilvray is an internationally respected Data Quality expert. She guides leaders and staff as they increase business value their organizations gain through Data Quality and Governance. This approach to data benefits focused initiatives (such as security, analytics, digital transformation, artificial intelligence, data science, and compliance).

Danette is the president and principal of Granite Falls Consulting, Inc., and is committed to the appropriate use of technology and to addressing the human aspects of data management through effective communication and change management.

Danette is the author of *Executing Data Quality Projects: Ten Steps to Quality Data and Trusted Information™*, 2nd Ed. (Elsevier/Academic Press, 2021), which shares a proven method used successfully by multiple industries in many countries. Her book is often described as a "classic" or noted as one of the "top ten" data management books in social media conversations. She is a co-author of The Leader's Data Manifesto (see dataleaders.org) and has overseen its translation into 21 languages.

Given your extensive experience as a Data Quality consultant, how often do you find a well-defined horizontal Data Strategy guiding the data-related work and responding to business strategy in your customers' organizations?

When I am asked to help an organization with its data quality or governance needs, I often find one of two things:

- Pockets of data management in places throughout the organization but no horizontal Data Strategy

- An overarching horizontal Data Strategy (often newly defined), but with no practical steps for implementing that strategy

---

[45] Danette McGilvray https://www.linkedin.com/in/danette-mcgilvray-bb9b85/

In the first instance, creating a horizontal Data Strategy can bring together the work that is already being done. By doing so, the organization can gain synergy, coordinate efforts, make the best use of its resources, and stop duplicate work.

In the second instance, the "devil is in the details." A good implementation plan is necessary, and the right people with the right knowledge and skills must be involved. In addition, paying attention to the human factors usually makes the difference between a successful implementation or the Data Strategy ending up in the dust bin.

What do you think is the role of Data Strategy in the success or failure of a Data Quality program?

A horizontal and integrated Data Strategy provides the overarching framework into which a Data Quality program fits. This makes it easier to stand up and maintain a Data Quality program because all the capabilities, roles, processes, technology, etc. necessary for high-quality, trusted data have been identified and their relationships are clear. EVERYTHING to do with data must first start with the business needs of the organization – including a Data Strategy. By business needs I mean those things that are most important to the organization to provide products and services, satisfy customers, manage risk, increase business value, implement strategies, achieve goals, address issues, and take advantage of opportunities. No matter which aspect of data you are working with, know the business needs and the data that supports those needs.

I take a holistic view of data quality, meaning that every aspect of data management is for the purpose of high-quality, trusted data – whether addressing metadata, architecture, master data management, etc. Data quality means bringing together data, processes, people, and technology throughout the data life cycle. A holistic view also addresses the human factors, communications, and ethics – essential for building trust in the data. A Data Strategy should lead the way here.

If a Data Strategy does not exist, building a Data Quality program is possible but will be slower. All the pieces mentioned still must work together for that data to meet business needs. Having a Data Strategy streamlines building a Data Quality program. A Data Strategy is foundational and long-term, which increases the chances that the various pieces of that strategy (including a Data Quality program) will continue to be funded and get proper attention.

From your perspective, who do you think should drive the creation and maintenance of a Data Strategy, and which stakeholders need to participate in this process?

A Chief Data Officer (CDO) is in the best position to drive the creation and maintenance of a Data Strategy. This assumes that the CDO is in an executive or very senior leader role within the organization. The CDO should be accountable for the Data Strategy and ensure support from other executives and the board of directors. The CDO may delegate some of the responsibility to lead the strategy and facilitate input from stakeholders. These responsible roles may vary within an organization but could include the most senior enterprise data roles within data governance, data quality, and/or data management.

As mentioned, we only care about data because it supports business needs. Because of this, it is essential to include executives and/or senior leaders from various business functions.

Managing data is not possible without the right information technology, so it is also crucial that the right executives and/or senior leaders from the Information Technology (IT) group are part of developing the strategy.

A well-run data governance process can enable the creation and maintenance of a Data Strategy – where those who have the authority to make decisions and those with the knowledge to make good decisions are brought together (representing business, data, and technology perspectives).

How would you recommend a new Data Governance lead create awareness and get buy-in from Senior Management on the relevance of building an integral and horizontal Data Strategy as the foundation for a successful Data Management program?

To create awareness and buy-in for a Data Strategy, it is all about the "Why?" Why should I care? Why is this important? Take the time to gather relevant examples to show "What's In It For Them" (WIIFT) if they support a Data Strategy. There are a number of what I call business impact techniques that can help here. To name a few: gathering anecdotes and telling the story that makes data and Data Strategy come alive to your audience; "connect the dots" between data, the role of Data Strategy, and business needs; show the risk of not having a Data Strategy, etc.

Find those who already understand the importance of good data. They are often those who have already felt the pain of poor-quality data and seen how the lack of high-quality data has undermined their business plans.

Work first with those who want to work with you. Your successes will bring in others who can participate later. If you have a vocal opponent, understand their opposition. They may have legitimate concerns that you can address. Find others that can influence those challengers or at least get them to stop shouting.

Cultivate your network of data-friendly partners or allies – at all levels of the organization. Give them the words to communicate, encourage them to listen, and request actions from their own networks. You cannot reach everyone yourself.

Develop communications/awareness/change management plans and implement them. Work with others in your organization who have those skills. Remember that working with people and addressing the human factors (have I emphasized this enough?) is not something that gets in the way of your Data Strategy work – it is an integral part of your work. And it is necessary for your success!

7.8.　　Closing Message

This work was inspired by insightful books and by experts in the field of Data Management. If it can now become a source of inspiration for you, writing it will have been worth it!

I encourage you to visit the book's companion website to find templates, study cases, examples of canvases, and more.

7.9.　　Companion Web Site

In this companion site you will find:

- Some images from the book
- Templates ready to use
- Samples of filled canvases
- Resources related to the book's topic
- A place to leave your comments/Testimonials/Experience using The Data Strategy PAC Method

https://segda.mx/

Follow me:

https://www.linkedin.com/in/marilul/

marilu.lopez@segda.com.mx

https://segda.com.mx/

Glossary

This section lists the most relevant terms used in this book, the meaning of which it is important to have clear. The convention followed here is that italics represent the definition taken from the indicated source, while regular font represents the meaning within this book.

Agile	*Able to move quickly and easily (Source: Oxford Dictionary).* Characteristic of the Data Strategy PAC Method to allow quick production of Data Strategies in an easy way.
Artifact	*An object that is made by a person (Source: Oxford Dictionary).* Any object that could be used as evidence of a practice being established. Used to prove the level of maturity as part of a Data Management Maturity Assessment, based on evidence. An Artifact can be a document, email distribution list, minutes, process documentation, etc.
Business Strategic Objectives	The highest-level steering statements to guide an organization/enterprise, are done as part of a plan to achieve business achievements.
Canvas	A piece of canvas (a strong, heavy, rough material used for making tents, sails, etc.) used for painting on (Source: Oxford Dictionary). A single slide where complex ideas or concepts are synthetized in way that makes them easy to understand; a Business Model Canvas, a Data Management Canvas.
Capability	Capability (to do something/of doing something) the ability or qualities necessary to do something (Source: Oxford Dictionary). Ability to execute a specific action, normally around processes. A capability is something that can be established as part of the business as usual (e.g., a process, a set of policies, a set of roles definition and designation, etc.)
Communicable	*That someone can communicate to someone else an idea (Source: Oxford Dictionary).* A characteristic of the Data Strategy PAC Method that makes it easy to read and understand.
Communication Channels	All the means to transmit a message within an organization/enterprise. Can be physical or electronic bulletin boards, share spaces, email, meet and lunch, town hall meetings, etc.
Critical Data Element	*A data element that is aligned to a critical business element and is deemed materially important (Source EDMC DCAM).* Critical Data Element or CDE is the one that when it does not meet the required data quality levels, can create an operational, financial, or reputational impact.

Data	Represents facts about the world and is a relevant asset for the organization (Source: DMBoK 2)
Data Asset	Any entity that is comprised of data. For example, a database is a data asset that is comprised of data records. A data asset may be a system or application output file, database, document, or web page. A data asset also includes a service that may be provided to access data from an application. For example, a service that returns individual records from a database would be a data asset. Similarly, a web site that returns data in response to specific queries (e.g., www.weather.com) would be a data asset. (Source: NIST CSRC)
Data Consumers	Any person, team, or system that uses data. The term is used to distinguish between data producers (who create data) and those who use data. A data consumer for one process may be a data producer for another process. (Source: (Sebastian-Coleman, 2022))
Data Domain	A logical grouping of data describing things that are relevant to the organization (customers, products, employees, etc.)
Data Governance	The exercise of authority, control, and shared decision-making (planning, monitoring, and enforcement) over the management of data assets (Source: Data Governance Institute, Gwen Thomas)
Data Governance Capabilities	Set of capacities to establish the practice of Data Governance (e.g., Data Governance Strategy defined, roles and responsibilities defined, funding process established, etc.)
Data Governance Practice	Continuous execution of the Data Governance capabilities.
Data Governance Strategic Objectives	Highest level statements to guide the implementation and execution of the Data Governance practice.
Data Management	The development, execution, and supervision of plans, policies, programs, and practices that deliver, control, protect and enhance the value of data and information assets throughout their lifecycles (Source: DMBoK 2)
Data Management Functions	Each of the different disciplines that together, working in a cohesive way, represent the Data Management function (Data Governance, Data Architecture, Data Modeling, Data Storage, Data Security, Data Integration, Document and Content Management, Master and Reference Data, Data Warehousing, Metadata Management and Data Quality Management)

Data Management Strategic Objectives	The highest-level statements to guide a Data Management program.
Data pain-point	Negative impacts in the organization, derived from issues related to data.
Data Principles	*Principle: a law, a rule, or a theory that something is based on (Source: Oxford Dictionary).* Data Principles are those rules defined in Data Alignment Strategy to guide the behavior of people within the organization in relation to data assets.
Data Providers	Internal organizational units or external entities (organizations/enterprises) producing data.
Data Strategies	The highest-level guidance in an organization on intelligently assigning resources to work in an integrated way to achieve data-related goals and contribute to achieving business strategic objectives.
Data Strategy Cycle	Third component of The Data Strategy PAC Method, comprised of ten steps to go from defining the scope and audience involved in defining the Data Strategies, going through the production of each different type of Data Strategies, communicating them, and ending with the integration with the enterprise strategic planning. This is an annual cycle to maintain Data Strategy aligned with the enterprise strategy.
Data-related behaviors	Systematic actions people involved with data do that do not benefit a Data Management practice and a sound Data Culture.
Design Thinking	Design thinking is a non-linear, iterative process that teams use to understand users, challenge assumptions, redefine problems and create innovative solutions to prototype and test. Involving five phases—Empathize, Define, Ideate, Prototype and Test—it is most useful to tackle problems that are ill-defined or unknown. (Source: Interaction Design Foundation)
Domain	The complete set of all possible values that an attribute can be assigned. (Source: (Hoberman, 2016))
Enterprise Strategy	The highest-level guidance to operate a business.
Entity	A collection of information about something that the business deems important and worthy of capture. A noun or noun phrase identifies a specific entity. It fits into one of several categories: who, what, when, where, why, or how. (Source: (Hoberman, 2016))
Large business/organization	More than 1500 employees or volunteers. Local or multi-national presence.

Medium business/organization	More than 50 employees or volunteers and less than 1,500. Local or multi-national presence.
Partners	Organizational units or stakeholders that based on their role in the organization their reliance on data are good allies for the Data Management program.
PAC	Pragmatic, Agile and Communicable. Characteristics of the Data Strategy Method described in this book.
PMO	*Project Management Office.* Normally, a good candidate to become a partner of Data Governance team.
Pragmatic	Solving problems in a practical and sensible way rather than by having fixed ideas or theories. (Source: Oxford Dictionary)
Small business/organization	50 or fewer employees or volunteers.
Socialize	To meet with someone to communicate an idea, proposal, initiative or the progress of an ongoing effort.
Strategic Initiative	A program (set of projects) with sponsorship and visibility at the highest level in the organization (e.g., merging and acquisition, digital or cultural transformation, new system acquisition, systems migration, etc.)
Strategy	Strategy is the **highest-level guidance** available to an organization, focusing activities on **articulated goal achievement** and providing direction and specific guidance when faced with a stream of decisions or uncertainties (Source: (Aiken & Harbour, 2017))

Bibliography

Aiken, P., & Harbour, T. (2017). *Data Strategy and the Enterprise Data Executive.* Technics Publications.

Alexander Osterwalder. (2005). *Canvas.* Retrieved from Strategyzer: https://www.strategyzer.com/canvas

Britannica Dictionary. (2022). Retrieved from https://www.britannica.com/dictionary/capability

DAMA International. (2010,). *Data Management Dictionary.* Retrieved from DAMA International: Https://dama.org

DAMA International. (2017). *Data Management Body of Knowledge.* Technics Publications.

DAMA International. (2017). *The DAMA Guide to the Data Management Body of Knowledge (DAM A-DM BOK).* Bradley Beach, NJ: Technics Publications, LLC.

Data Literacy Project. (2021). *The Seven Principles of Data Literacy.*

DATAVERSITY. (2021, October 12). Retrieved from Data Topics: https://www.dataversity.net/data-management-vs-data-strategy-a-framework-for-business-success/

Edvinsson, H. (2020). *Data Diplomacy.* New Jersey: Technics Publications.

Edvinsson, H. (2020). *Data Diplomacy.* New Jersey: Technics Publications.

Enterprise Data Management Council. (2021). *DCAM Data Management Capability Assessment Model 2.2.* EDM Council.

Gartner Group. (2018). Getting Started With Data Literacy and Information as a Second Language: A Gartner Trend Insight Report.

Geeks for Geeks. (2021, November). *Geeks for Geeks What is Semi-structured data?* Retrieved from Geeks for Geeks: https://www.geeksforgeeks.org/what-is-semi-structured-data/

Hoberman, S. (2016). *Data Modeling Made Simple.* New Jersey: Technics Publications, LLC.

Inmon, W., Lindstedt, D., & Levins, M. (2019). *Data Architecture A Primer for the Data Scientist Second Edition.* London: Elsevier.

Knight, M. (2021). *What is Data Strategy.* Los Angeles, California: DATAVERSITY.

Manifesto, T. L. (2016). *Leader's Data Manifesto.* Retrieved from Dataleaders.og: https://dataleaders.org/manifesto/

Merrian Webster Dictionary. (2022). *Merriam Webster Dictionary - Capability.* Retrieved from Merriam Webster Dictionary: https://www.merriam-webster.com/dictionary/capability

Plotkin, D. (2021). *Data Stewardship, second edition.* London: Elsevier.

Sebastian-Coleman, L. (2022). *Meeting the Challenges of Data Quality Management.* London: Elsevier.

Seiner, R. S. (2014). *Npn-Invasive Data Governance.* Basking Ridge, NJ: Technics Publications, LLC.

Simon, H. (2019). The Sciences of the Artificial Third Edition. Boston: The MIT Press.

Stadler, C., Hautz, J., Matzler, K., & Friedrich von den Eichen, S. (2021). *OPEN STRATEGY: Mastering Disruption From Outside the C-suite.* London: England.

TechTarget. (2022). *What is digital transformation?* Retrieved from Techtarget Search CIO: https://www.techtarget.com/searchcio/definition/digital-transformation

Wallis, I. (2021). Data Strategy: from definition to execution. BCS.

Wikipedia. (2022). *Digital Transformation.* Retrieved from Wikipedia English: https://en.wikipedia.org/wiki/Digital_transformation

Index